J'écoute, je joue & j'apprends

ÂGE 8+

L'ANGLAIS

À mes trois fils et à la vraie Georgia, qui a inspiré le personnage de ce livre.
K. H.

Merci à David Warner, la source de mon inspiration.
S. T.

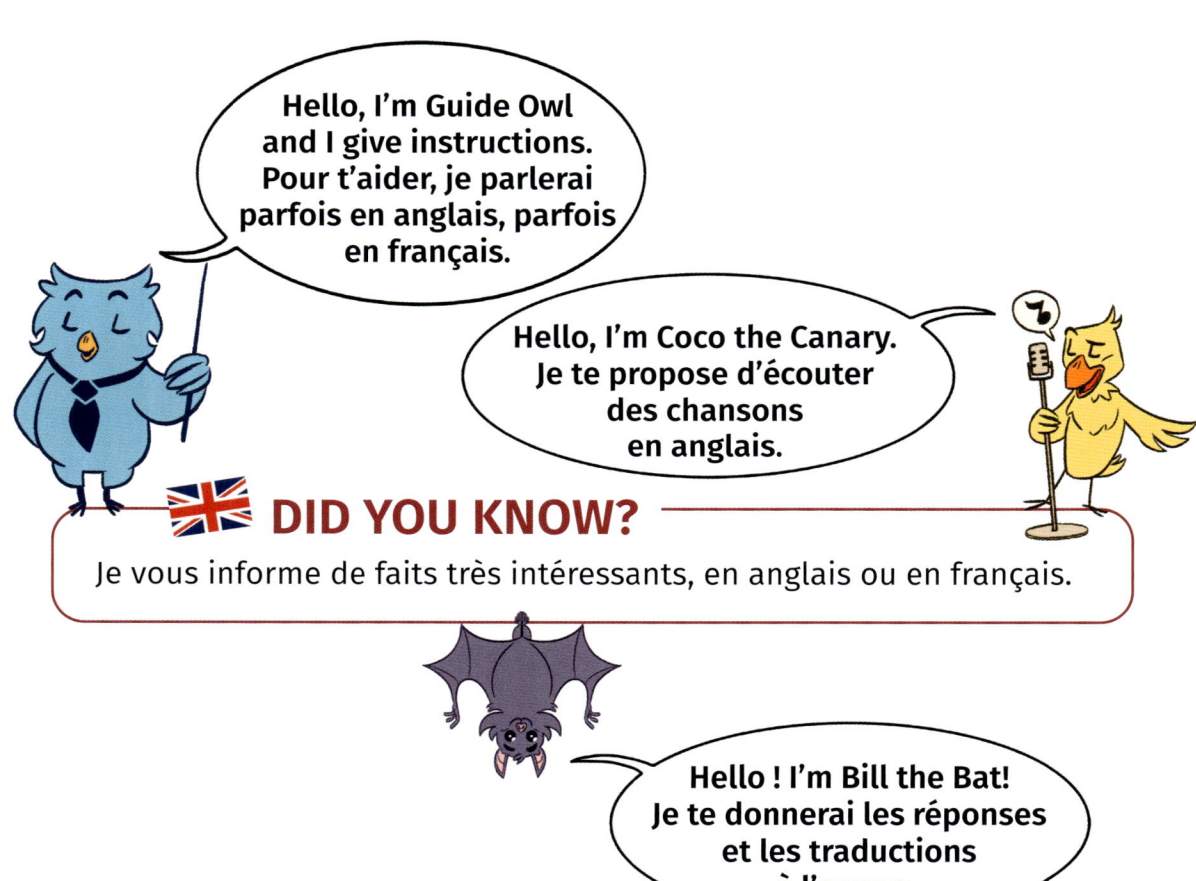

assimil
KIDS & TEENS

J'écoute, je joue & j'apprends L'ANGLAIS

ÂGE 8+

Kate Holiday • Sarah Tirard
Illustrations : Maud Liénard • SaruJin

Welcome to Sealand!

Bienvenue dans une petite ville du comté de Dorset, sur la côte sud-ouest de l'Angleterre. Un beau jour d'été, quelque chose de grave se passe dans la maison où vit Ruby, la chienne border collie…

COMIC STRIP

Dans la case 1, Ruby dit : « Je vais t'attraper ! » Dans la case 2, « Grrr ! Ces chats ! » Dans la case 3, « Je suis perdue ! »

Comment Ruby va-t-elle retrouver sa famille ? Mets-toi à sa place et réfléchis à ce que tu pourrais faire. Sûrement trouver des gens ou des animaux gentils qui voudront bien t'aider. Ils parleront en anglais ou en français, et c'est comme ça que tu vas progresser dans ton enquête… et en anglais !

CLUE

Tu vas aider Ruby à retrouver sa famille. Trouve un indice dans chaque chapitre de ce livre pour découvrir sa nouvelle adresse. Note-le sur le carnet à la dernière page du livre. Il n'est pas obligatoire de le faire dans l'ordre. Good luck!

VOCABULARY

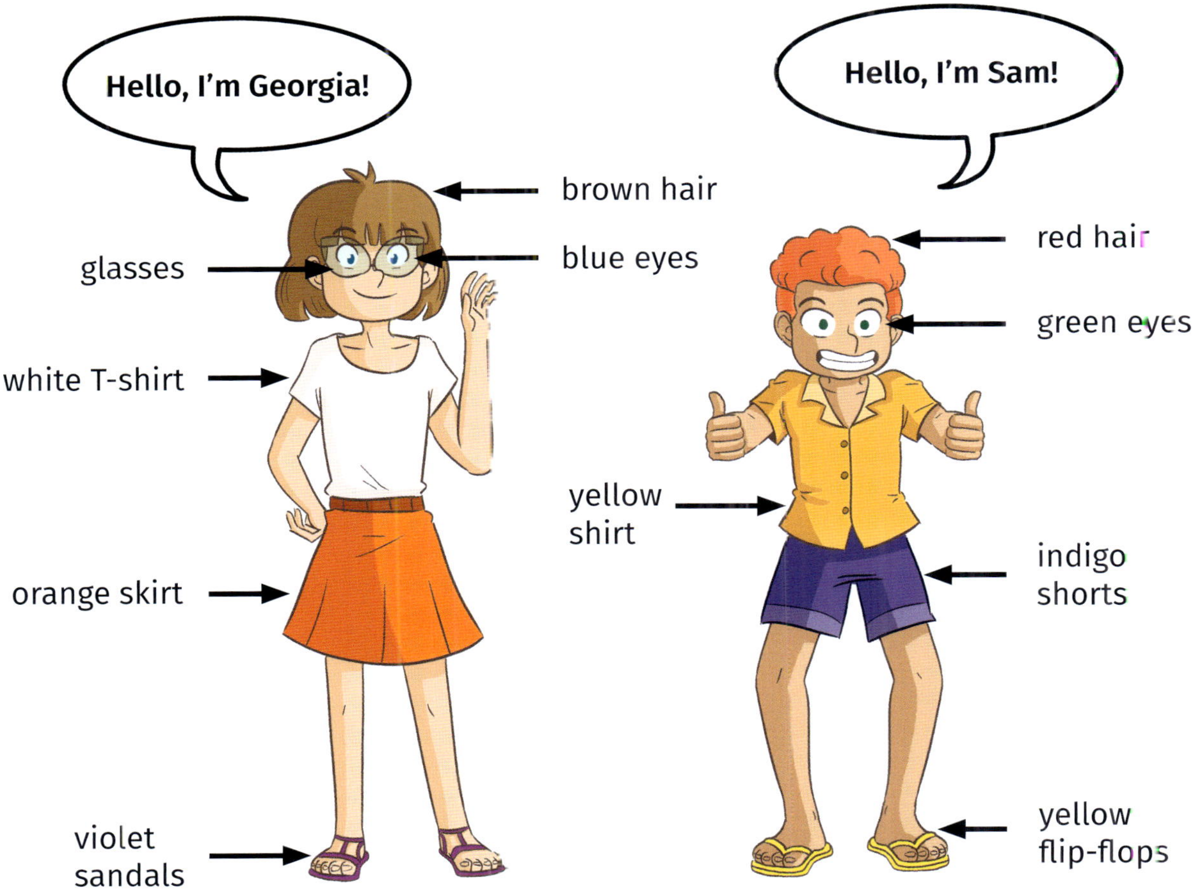

Hello, I'm Georgia!

- brown hair
- blue eyes
- glasses
- white T-shirt
- orange skirt
- violet sandals

Hello, I'm Sam!

- red hair
- green eyes
- yellow shirt
- indigo shorts
- yellow flip-flops

Choose Your Destination!

Choisis ta première destination !

2 **The Sweetshop**
Go to page 16

10 **Activity Centre**
Go to page 76

5 **The Wildlife Park**
Go to page 40

7 **The Old Castle**
Go to page 54

3 **Georgia's House**
Go to page 26

4 The Toyshop
Go to page 34

6 The General Store
Go to page 48

1 The Park
Go to page 10

8 The Funfair
Go to page 60

9 The Beach
Go to page 68

1 The Park

LET'S PLAY!

WHAT COLOUR?

- What colour are Sam's shorts?
- What colour are Georgia's eyes?
- What colour is Sam's shirt?
- What colour is Georgia's skirt?
- What colour is Guide Owl?

Sam's shorts are indigo. / Georgia's eyes are blue. / Sam's shirt is yellow. / Georgia's skirt is orange. / Guide Owl is blue.

1 • The Park

DIALOGUE

Sam: Look Georgia, there's a dog! Listen Georgia, there's an owl!

Georgia: Come on Sam, let's go and look! The dog is going to see the owl!

Sam: Look, the owl is giving a mysterious map to the dog.

Sam : Regarde, Georgia, il y a un chien ! Écoute Georgia, il y a une chouette.
Georgia : Viens, Sam, allons regarder ! Le chien va voir la chouette !
Sam : Regarde, la chouette donne une carte mystérieuse au chien.

COMIC STRIP

I'm lost!

Ruby catches the map.

Case 1 : Ruby attrape la carte.
Dans la case 3, Ruby dit : « Je suis perdue ! »

LET'S PLAY!

TRUE OR FALSE?

❶ Georgia has red hair.
❷ Sam has green eyes.
❸ Ruby is a Border Collie.
❹ Guide Owl is blue.
❺ Georgia has a violet skirt.

1F / 2T / 3T / 4T / 5F.

Ruby Can Talk by Magic!

Ruby's magic map

DIALOGUE

Ruby: Can you help me, children?

Georgia: You can talk, wow! Are you a magic dog?

Ruby: No, this is a magic map. I can talk when I touch the map.

Georgia: That's magic! What's your name?

Ruby: My name is Ruby and I'm three. What's your name?

Georgia: My name is Georgia and I'm ten years old. This is Sam, he is nine years old.

Ruby: Hello!

Georgia: How can we help you, Ruby?

Ruby: Please help me find my new home.

Ruby : Pouvez-vous m'aider, les enfants ?
Georgia : Tu sais parler ! Wouah ! Es-tu un chien magique ?
Ruby : Non, mais la carte est magique. Je peux parler quand je touche la carte.
Georgia : C'est magique ! Comment t'appelles-tu ?
Ruby : Je m'appelle Ruby et j'ai 3 ans. Comment t'appelles-tu ?
Georgia : Je m'appelle Georgia et j'ai 10 ans. Voici Sam, qui a 9 ans.
Ruby : Bonjour !
Georgia : Que pouvons-nous faire pour t'aider, Ruby ?
Ruby : Aidez-moi à trouver ma nouvelle maison, s'il vous plaît.

1 • The Park

LET'S PLAY!

WORDSEARCH

⭐ Find the colours of the rainbow!
Words to find: rainbow / red / orange / yellow / green / blue / indigo / violet.

R	A	I	N	B	O	W	X	I	L	O
E	E	D	N	A	A	E	N	N	S	R
L	K	G	R	E	E	N	B	D	L	A
I	W	W	O	W	B	N	H	I	L	N
B	L	U	E	E	D	N	B	G	S	G
E	S	E	G	N	A	R	O	O	N	E
M	U	S	H	O	Y	E	R	S	Y	T
V	I	O	L	E	T	Z	K	L	N	O
I	S	L	S	R	N	O	S	V	E	R
V	H	E	S	B	L	S	E	R	I	G
T	I	O	G	L	N	N	S	E	L	U
G	N	B	R	E	N	L	O	D	L	A
I	E	Y	E	L	L	O	W	D	D	E

Clue Time

VOCABULARY

rainy sunny snowy

CLUE

L'indice numéro 1 est le mot anglais qui signifie « ensoleillé ». Inscris-le dans le carnet d'adresses, à la fin du livre.

Clue 1

COMIC STRIP

Well done! Now go and find another clue!

Off we go!

Dans la case 1, Guide Owl dit : « Bravo ! Allez maintenant trouver un autre indice ! »
Dans la case 3, Guide Owl dit : « Allons-y ! »

1 • The Park

LET'S SING

I CAN SING A RAINBOW

Red and yellow and pink and green, orange and purple and blue
I can sing a rainbow, sing a rainbow, you can sing one too
Listen with your eyes
Listen with your heart
And sing everything you see
You can sing a rainbow, sing a rainbow, sing along with me
Red and yellow and pink and green, orange and purple and blue
I can sing a rainbow, sing a rainbow, you can sing one too.

Je peux chanter un arc-en-ciel
Rouge et jaune et rose et vert, orange et violet et bleu
Je chante l'arc-en-ciel, chante l'arc-en-ciel, tu peux le chanter aussi.
Écoute avec tes yeux
Écoute avec ton cœur
Chante tout ce que tu vois
Tu peux chanter l'arc-en-ciel, chanter l'arc-en-ciel, chanter avec moi.
Rouge et jaune et rose et vert, orange et violet et bleu
Je chante l'arc-en-ciel, chante l'arc-en-ciel, tu peux le chanter aussi.

🇬🇧 DID YOU KNOW?

Le *goody bag* est un petit sac rempli de bonbons, gâteaux et cadeaux avec lequel les enfants au Royaume-Uni repartent d'un goûter d'anniversaire.

Est-ce que tu connais chacun de ces mots anglais ? Est-ce que tu connais aussi le mot qui correspond à chacun de ces dessins ? Si oui bravo, si non, retourne au début du chapitre pour réviser.

2 The Sweetshop

DIALOGUE

chocolate

toffee

chocolate buttons

Georgia: Ruby, I'm sorry, you can't come inside the shop. You are a dog. Dogs can't come into sweetshops. Wait for us outside. Poor Ruby!

Mrs Brown: Hello, children. What would you like?

Georgia: Hello, Mrs Brown. I have some pocket money. I would like to buy some sweets, please.

Mrs Brown: Look! On the left, there are sweets and, on the right, there are chocolates.

Georgia: Please can I have some jelly babies?

Mrs Brown: Here you are. One pound, please.

Georgia: Here you are. Thank you. Goodbye!

Mrs Brown: Goodbye!

sweets

jelly baby

fruit pastilles

2 • The Sweetshop

Geo*rg*ia : Ruby, je suis désolée. Tu ne peux pas rentrer dans le magasin. Tu es un chien. Les chiens ne doivent pas *entrer dans les magasins de bonbons. Attends-nous dehors. Pauvre Ruby !
M*rs* Brown : Bonjour les enfants. Que voulez-vous ?
Georgia : Bonjour Madame Brown, j'ai de l'argent de poche. Je voudrais acheter des bonbons, s'il vous plaît.
M*rs* Brown : Regardez ! À gauche, il y a des bonbons et à droite, il y a des chocolats.
Georgia : Puis-je avoir des jelly babies, s'il vous plaît ?
M*r*s Brown : Voici. Une livre, s'il te plaît.
Georgia : Voici. Merci et au revoir !
M*rs* Brown : Au revoir !

GRAMMAR

POINT OUT

En anglais, quand tu veux dire « il y a un chien », tu dis "there is a dog".
S'il y en a deux, tu dis "there are two dogs".

There is
There is a dog
on the table.

There isn't
There isn't a cat
on the table.

Is there?
Is there a cat or a dog
on the table?

There are
There are two dogs
on the table.

There aren't
There aren't two dogs
on the table.

Are there?
Are there two dogs
on the table?

Outside the Sweetshop

COMIC STRIP

VOCABULARY

Je vais te montrer quelque chose de chouette qui va t'aider en anglais. De nombreux mots se composent de deux mots, par exemple, "pocket money" (argent de poche). Tu vas en voir beaucoup dans ce livre.

 +  = pocket money

 +  = jelly baby

 +  = fruit pastilles

Argent de poche / bonbon en gélatine / bonbons aux fruits.

2 • The Sweetshop

LET'S PLAY!

WORDSEARCH

⭐ Find the names of the sweets.

⭐ Words to find: toffee / lollipop / fudge / mints / jelly babies.

J	E	L	L	Y	B	A	B	I	E	S
G	Y	X	O	J	B	R	Z	V	K	M
W	V	B	L	N	O	T	R	N	X	O
N	R	Z	L	X	Y	E	F	Z	U	F
F	B	M	I	N	T	S	R	O	A	M
U	W	R	P	N	V	Z	X	N	K	X
D	Q	C	O	Z	T	O	F	F	E	E
G	K	Z	P	K	Z	N	I	R	C	F
E	Y	C	W	Z	F	G	N	B	V	X

🇬🇧 DID YOU KNOW?

En 1918, les *jelly babies* s'appelaient "*peace babies*" (bébés de la paix) pour commémorer la fin de la Première Guerre mondiale : ils sont alors devenus très populaires. Leur nom actuel ne date que des années 50.

Let's count!

2 • The Sweetshop

QUESTIONS

1. What is there in square 15?
2. What is there in square 11?
3. What is there in square 18?
4. What is there in square 21?
5. What is there in square 27?
6. What is there in square 34?
7. What is there in square 41?
8. What is there in square 46?
9. What is there in square 52?
10. What is there in square 56?
11. What is there in square 60?

1. A red lollipop / 2. Blue shorts / 3. A rainbow / 4. A pound / 5. Rain / 6. 2 jelly babies / 7. A tree / 8. A sun / 9. Chocolate / 10. 2 mints / 11. Fudge.

VOCABULARY

1 one	17 seventeen	33 thirty-three	49 forty-nine
2 two	18 eighteen	34 thirty-four	50 fifty
3 three	19 nineteen	35 thirty-five	51 fifty-one
4 four	20 twenty	36 thirty-six	52 fifty-two
5 five	21 twenty-one	37 thirty-seven	53 fifty-three
6 six	22 twenty-two	38 thirty-eight	54 fifty-four
7 seven	23 twenty-three	39 thirty-nine	55 fifty-five
8 eight	24 twenty-four	40 forty	56 fifty-six
9 nine	25 twenty-five	41 forty-one	57 fifty-seven
10 ten	26 twenty-six	42 forty-two	58 fifty-eight
11 eleven	27 twenty-seven	43 forty-three	59 fifty-nine
12 twelve	28 twenty-eight	44 forty-four	60 sixty
13 thirteen	29 twenty-nine	45 forty-five	61 sixty-one
14 fourteen	30 thirty	46 forty-six	62 sixty-two
15 fifteen	31 thirty-one	47 forty-seven	63 sixty-three
16 sixteen	32 thirty-two	48 forty-eight	64 sixty-four

Clue Time

COMIC STRIP

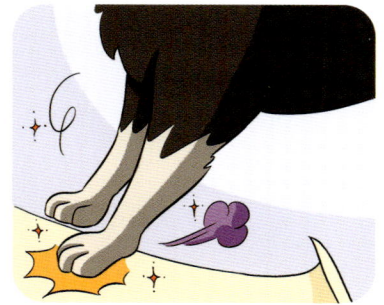

Dans la case 1, Georgia dit : « Montre-nous où aller maintenant ! »
Dans la case 3, Ruby dit : « Nous devons aller chez toi, Georgia ! »

VOCABULARY

CLUE

Where is the blue square on the box? Top or _ _ _ _?
Find clue number 2 and write it in the address book at the end of this book.

Où se trouve le carré bleu sur la boîte ? En haut ou _ _ _ _ ? Trouve l'indice numéro 2 et écris-le dans le carnet d'adresses à la fin du livre.

2 • The Sweetshop

LET'S SING

SWEET SONG

Sweets, sweets, I love sweets
Donuts, ice cream
Chocolate, candy, pudding, cake
What's your favourite sweet?

Sweets, sweets, I love sweets
Donuts, ice cream
Chocolate, candy, pudding, cake
What's your favourite sweet?

Chanson sucrée
Les bonbons, les bonbons, j'aime les bonbons
Les donuts, les glaces
Le chocolat, les bonbons, les desserts, les gâteaux
C'est quoi, ton bonbon préféré ?

Les bonbons, les bonbons, j'aime les bonbons
Les donuts, et les glaces
Le chocolat, les bonbons, les desserts, les gâteaux
C'est quoi, ton bonbon préféré ?

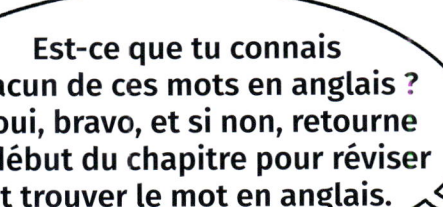

Est-ce que tu connais chacun de ces mots en anglais ? Si oui, bravo, et si non, retourne au début du chapitre pour réviser et trouver le mot en anglais.

hello · there is · please · can't · outside · sweetshop · thank you · inside · there are · can · goodbye

Learning Prepositions

 VOCABULARY

Look at this to help you before you do scene 3.

PLACE AND MOVEMENT

24

2 • The Sweetshop

PLACE AND MOVEMENT

EXPRESSION

1. I like chasing cats around the tree.

2. I like chasing cats across the park.

4. Grrr, the cats are coming towards me!

5. Grrr, one cat is in front of the tree and the second cat is behind the tree!

3. Oh no, now the two cats are up the tree!

1. J'ai me chasser les chats autour de l'arbre.
2. J'aime chasser les chats à travers le parc.
3. Oh non, maintenant les deux chats ont grimpé dans l'arbre !
4. Grrr, les chats viennent vers moi !
5. Grrr, un des chats est devant l'arbre et l'autre chat est derrière l'arbre !

3 Georgia's House

DIALOGUE

Mum: Hello Georgia, who is this?

Georgia: Hello Mum! This is Sam, my friend, and this is Ruby. Ruby is lost. We must help her find her family.

Mum: Hello Sam, hello Ruby. Nice to meet you.

Georgia: Yes, Ruby, you can come in. Look, this is my house. Come and visit the rooms.

Maman : Bonjour Georgia, qui est-ce ?

Georgia : Coucou, Maman. Voici Sam, mon ami, et voici Ruby. Ruby est perdue. Nous devons l'aider à retrouver sa famille.

Maman : Bonjour Sam, bonjour Ruby. Je suis heureuse de vous rencontrer.

Georgia : Oui, Ruby, tu peux rentrer.

Georgia : Regardez, c'est ma maison. Venez visiter les pièces.

VOCABULARY

Voici une maison de campagne typiquement anglaise : on l'appelle « a cottage ».

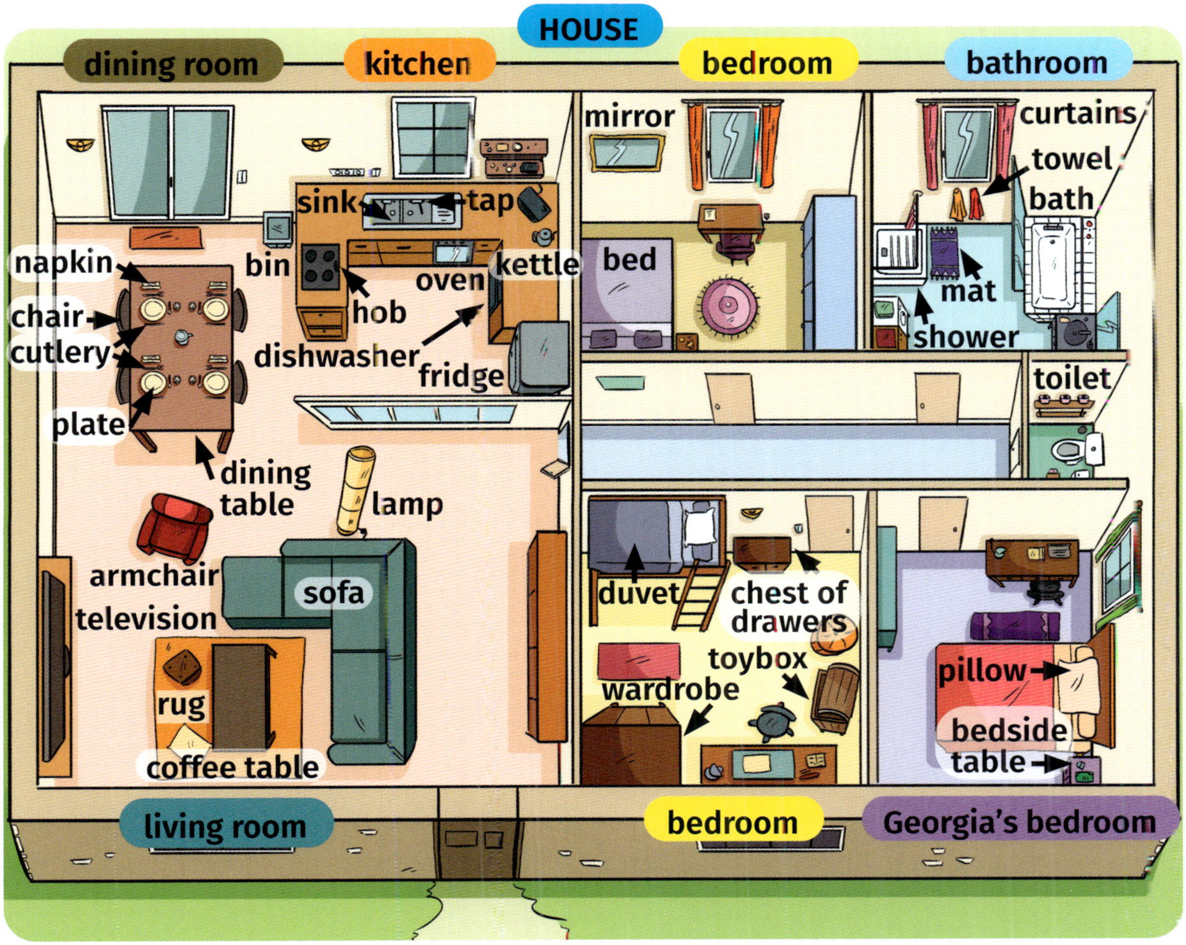

3 • Georgia's House

HOUSE

Labelled floor plan showing:
- **dining room**: napkin, chair, cutlery, plate, dining table
- **kitchen**: sink, tap, bin, oven, hob, kettle, dishwasher, fridge
- **living room**: lamp, armchair, television, sofa, rug, coffee table
- **bedroom**: mirror, bed
- **bathroom**: curtains, towel, bath, mat, shower, toilet
- **bedroom**: duvet, chest of drawers, toybox, wardrobe
- **Georgia's bedroom**: pillow, bedside table

LET'S PLAY!

TRUE OR FALSE?

❶ The bathroom is in the kitchen.
❷ There are two toilets in the bathroom.
❸ Georgia's bedroom is in the garden.
❹ Georgia lives in a house.
❺ The sink is in the living room.
❻ The curtains in Georgia's bedroom are green.

1F / 2F / 3F / 4T / 5F / 6T.

In the House

VOCABULARY

Voici encore des mots composés de deux mots.

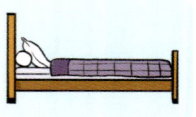 +  = bedroom

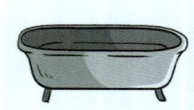 +  = bathroom

Chambre / salle de bain.

DIALOGUE

Georgia: Come on, Sam and Ruby, let's go to my bedroom to play.

Sam: Great idea. I'd like to play cards.

Georgia: Don't worry, Ruby, I have a ball you can play with.

Ruby: Don't forget, we mustn't be long, we have to find more clues.

Georgia: Yes, I know, we'll play a quick game. Oh, listen, it's Mum! She's calling us.

Georgia : Venez, Sam et Ruby, allons dans ma chambre pour jouer.
Sam : Super idée. J'aimerais jouer aux cartes.
Georgia : Ne t'inquiète pas, Ruby, j'ai un ballon pour toi.
Ruby : N'oubliez-pas que nous devons trouver d'autres indices, il ne faut pas trop tarder.
Georgia : Oui, je sais, on va faire un jeu rapide. Oh, écoutez, c'est maman ! Elle nous appelle.

3 • Georgia's House

COMIC STRIP

DIALOGUE

Mum: Come and sit down. Would you like a drink? Would you like a biscuit?

Georgia: Yes, Ruby. You can have a drink and a biscuit. Come on Sam, come on Ruby. We must find the new address of Ruby's family. Goodbye Mum, see you later.

Mum: Goodbye Georgia, goodbye Sam and goodbye Ruby.

Maman : Venez vous asseoir. Voulez-vous une boisson ? Voulez-vous un biscuit ?

Georgia : Oui, Ruby. Tu peux boire et avoir un biscuit. Merci, Maman. Viens Sam, viens Ruby. Nous devons trouver la nouvelle adresse de la famille de Ruby. Au revoir, Maman, à tout à l'heure.

Maman : Au revoir Georgia, au revoir Sam et au revoir Ruby.

Georgia's Bedroom

LET'S PLAY!

SPOT THE DIFFERENCES

⭐ Tu dois trouver les 8 différences entre les deux images de la chambre de Georgia.

⭐ Fais des phrases en anglais pour les citer.

There are three pairs of shoes under the bed.
The duvet on the bed is green.
The cushion on the chair is blue.
There are two books on the bedside table.
The teddy bear on the bed has a yellow hat.
There is a dinosaur on the chest of drawers.
There are four photos on the wall.
The curtains are blue.

3 • Georgia's House

VOCABULARY

Donne le nom anglais de chacun de ces meubles et objets, puis précise dans quelle pièce ils se trouvent. For example: The pillow goes in the bedroom. The towel goes in the bathroom.

first floor

ground floor

The toybox goes in the bedroom: just like the duvet, the pillow, the bedside table, the wardrobe, the chest of drawers, the bed and the rug.
The armchair goes in the living room: just like the sofa, the television and the coffee table.
The bath goes in the bathroom: just like the bathmat, the mirror, the shower, the tap, the towel and the toilet.
The fridge goes in the kitchen: just like the hob, the sink and the dishwasher.
The dining table goes in the dining room.

Clue Time

CLUE

Find clue number 3.
Where does Georgia live ?
Georgia lives in a _ _ _ _ _.

Clue 3

1. Georgia lives in a  (E-C-A-L-T-S)?

2. Georgia lives in a  (E-H-U-S-O)?

2. Georgia lives in a  (K-R-P-A)?

Trouve l'indice n° 3 : Où vit Georgia ? Georgia vit dans une…

LET'S SING

POLLY PUT THE KETTLE ON

Polly put the kettle on,
Polly put the kettle on,
Polly put the kettle on,
We'll all have tea.
Sukey take it off again,
Sukey take it off again,
Sukey take it off again,
They've all gone away.

Polly met la bouilloire en marche
Polly fait chauffer la bouilloire
Polly fait chauffer la bouilloire
Polly fait chauffer la bouilloire,
On va tous prendre le thé
Sukey, enlève-la de nouveau
Sukey, enlève-la de nouveau
Sukey, enlève-la, ils sont tous repartis.

3 • Georgia's House

🇬🇧 DID YOU KNOW?

On connaissait le goût des Britanniques pour le thé (ils en consomment 2,3 kg par an, par habitant !) mais voilà que les Français s'y mettent avec près de 250 g par an, par habitant.

Did you know a British person drinks 2.3 kgs of tea every year, but in France, each person drinks 250 g of tea?

Est-ce que tu connais chacun de ces mots anglais ? Est-ce que tu connais aussi le mot qui correspond à chacun de ces dessins ? Si oui bravo, si non, retourne au début du chapitre pour réviser.

BEDROOM — CHEST OF DRAWERS — WHO — DINING ROOM — MAP — LIVING ROOM — ROOM — DINING TABLE — RUG — WARDROBE — COME IN — HOB — TAP — BATHROOM — CUTLERY — BEDSIDE TABLE — NAPKIN — KITCHEN — DISHWASHER — A DRINK — COFFEE TABLE

4 The Toyshop

"Hello, I'm William. This is my toyshop!"

"Here we are in front of the toyshop. You must find clue number 4."

DIALOGUE

Georgia: Hello, William. How are you?

William: Hello, Georgia. I'm fine, thank you. Who's this?

Georgia: This is Sam, my friend.

Sam: Hello, William, nice to meet you.

William: There's a Border Collie outside the shop. Is this your dog, Georgia?

Georgia: No, Ruby isn't our dog but she's our friend. She's lost and we must help her find her family.

William: Sam, do you like the toys and the fancy dress costumes?

Sam: Oh yes, William! I love your shop. I would like to buy the football shirt with my pocket money. How much is it, please?

William: It costs 10 pounds, Sam. Here you are.

Georgia : Bonjour, William. Comment allez-vous ?

William : Bonjour, Georgia. Je vais très bien, merci. Qui est-ce ?

Georgia : C'est Sam, mon ami.

Sam : Bonjour William, heureux de faire votre connaissance.

William : Il y a un chien border collie devant le magasin. Est-ce que c'est ton chien, Georgia ?

Georgia : Non, Ruby n'est pas notre chien, mais c'est notre amie. Elle est perdue et nous devons l'aider à retrouver sa famille.

William : Sam, est-ce que tu aimes les jouets et les déguisements ?

Sam : Oh oui ! William. J'adore votre magasin. Je voudrais acheter le maillot de foot avec mon argent de poche. Combien coûte-t-il, s'il vous plaît ?

William : Il coûte 10 livres, Sam. Tiens !

4 • The Toyshop

COMIC STRIP

Dans la case 2, Ruby dit : « Ne passez pas trop de temps dans le magasin de jouets. »

VOCABULARY

Clue Time

COMIC STRIP

Dans la case 2, Georgia et Sam disent en même temps : « Au revoir William, merci beaucoup ! » Dans la case 3, William dit : « Bonne chance ! »

CLUE

What is the number on the football shirt? Write the answer in the address book at the end of this book.

Clue 4

Quel numéro est écrit sur le maillot de foot ? Écris-le dans le carnet d'adresses à la fin du livre.

LET'S PLAY!

TRUE OR FALSE?

1. Georgia buys a football kit.
2. Ruby comes inside the toyshop.
3. The salamander is yellow and black.
4. The spider is real.
5. The teddy bear is blue.

1F / 2F / 3T / 4F / 5T.

4 • The Toyshop

VOCABULARY

COMPOUND NOUNS

 +  = pushchair

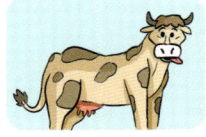 +  = cowboy

 +  = building brick

 + 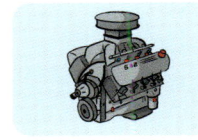 = fire engine

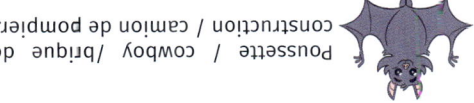
Poussette / cowboy / brique de construction / camion de pompier.

TONGUE TWISTERS

Essaie de dire cette phrase pendant 30 secondes, sans te tordre la langue : red lorry, yellow lorry, red lorry, yellow lorry.

DID YOU KNOW?

Did you know that in English, we have sentences called "tongue twisters". En français, cela veut dire « ce qui tord la langue », parce que, quand on essaie de les prononcer rapidement, on se tord la langue !

Song and Recap

LET'S SING

INCY WINCY SPIDER

Incy Wincy spider
Went up the water spout
Down came the rain
And washed poor Incy out
Out came the sunshine and dried up all the rain
And Incy Wincy spider
Went up the spout again.

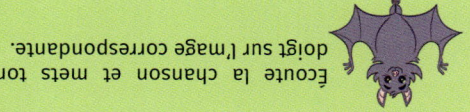 Listen to the song and point to the corresponding picture.

Écoute la chanson et mets ton doigt sur l'image correspondante.

Incy Wincy l'araignée
Incy Wincy l'araignée
Montait dans la gouttière
Voilà la pluie
La pauvre Incy est tombée par terre
Le soleil est sorti
Pour sécher toute la pluie
Et Incy Wincy l'araignée
Est remontée dans la gouttière.

🇬🇧 **DID YOU KNOW?**

En Grande-Bretagne, on n'utilise pas l'euro, mais la livre (« pound » en anglais).

4 • The Toyshop

LET'S PLAY!

TEST YOUR VOCABULARY

⭐ Relie chacune de ces expressions en anglais avec sa traduction en français.

1. How are you?
2. Is this your dog?
3. How much is it, please?
4. Wait outside!
5. Good luck!
6. Who is this?

A. Qui est-ce ?
B. Combien ça coûte, s'il vous plaît ?
C. Bonne chance !
D. Comment allez-vous ?
E. Attends dehors !
F. Est-ce votre chien ?

1D / 2F / 3B / 4E / 5C / 6A.

Est-ce que tu connais chacun de ces mots en anglais ? Si oui, bravo, et si non, retourne au début du chapitre pour réviser et trouver le mot en anglais.

BOOK · FRIEND · TO LOVE · TO COST · LORRY · TO BUY · TOY

5 The Wildlife Park

DIALOGUE

Sam: It's so windy!

Georgia: Oh no, the map, it's up in the tree!

Sam: Thank you Mrs Giraffe, you got the map with your long neck!

Georgia: Come on, Sam, let's go and look at the gorillas.

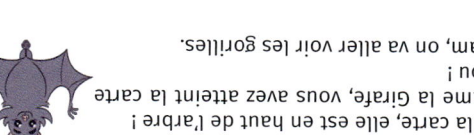

Sam : Il y a tellement de vent !
Georgia : Oh non, la carte, elle est en haut de l'arbre !
Sam : Merci Madame la Girafe, vous avez atteint la carte avec votre long cou !
Georgia : Viens, Sam, on va aller voir les gorilles.

5 • The Wildlife Park

COMIC STRIP

DIALOGUE

Ruby: Hello, wolf leader Nikko, my name is Ruby and I'm very happy to meet you.

Nikko: Hello, Ruby, you are a strange wolf. Why are you so small and black and white?

Ruby: Because I'm not a wolf, I'm a dog. Georgia, Sam and I are on a quest to find a clue here in the Wildlife Park. Do you know about a number we have to find?

Nikko: Hmm, I will ask the other wolves in my pack...

Ruby : Bonjour, Nikko le chef des loups, je m'appelle Ruby et je suis très heureuse de te rencontrer.

Nikko : Bonjour, Ruby, tu es un loup étrange. Pourquoi es-tu si petit, noir et blanc ?

Ruby : Parce que je ne suis pas un loup, je suis un chien. Georgia, Sam et moi sommes à la recherche d'un indice dans le parc animalier. Connais-tu un numéro que nous devons trouver ?

Nikko : Hmm, je vais demander aux autres loups de ma meute...

Nikko: So, my friend Ruby, the clue will be found in the camel paddock, the next paddock on the right! Lou, my friend, knows about the clue.

Ruby: Great! Thank you so much to you and Lou. Nice to meet you and have a good day!

Nikko: Goodbye, my friend Ruby.

Nikko : Alors, mon amie Ruby, l'indice se trouve dans l'enclos des chameaux, le prochain enclos à droite ! Lou, mon ami, connaît l'indice.

Ruby : Super ! Merci beaucoup à toi et à Lou. Ravi de vous avoir rencontrés et bonne journée !

Nikko : Au revoir, mon ami Ruby.

Clue Time

COMIC STRIP

Dans la case 2, Sam dit : « Allez-vous-en, les chats ! »
Dans la case 3, Georgia dit : « Parle, s'il te plaît ! »

DIALOGUE

Ruby: Georgia, Sam, we have to hurry now as it's getting late and we need to find the next clue. Nikko the Wolf says it is near the camel paddock. Let's go!

Georgia: Of course, Ruby, let's go straight away.

Ruby : Georgia, Sam, nous devons nous dépêcher maintenant car il se fait tard et nous devons trouver le prochain indice. Nikko le loup dit qu'il est près de l'enclos des chameaux. Allons-y !
Georgia : Bien sûr Ruby, allons-y tout de suite.

5 • The Wildlife Park

DIALOGUE

Georgia: Oh wow, what big camels! They have two humps on their back! The camels I know have only one hump. Ruby, can you ask them about the clue?

Ruby: Excuse me, Mister Camel, my friends and I are looking for a clue we need to find urgently. Do you have any information for us?

Mr. Camel: Hello, young dog, I don't know about a clue and I'm very tired and have to go now. Good luck!

Ruby: Oh, that's a shame! Thanks anyway, goodbye.

Georgia: Well, Ruby, what did he say?

Ruby: Nothing, absolutely nothing.

Georgia: Oh dear, this adventure is very difficult and we have to go home now.

Ruby: I'm sad Georgia, and Sam is sad, too.

Georgia : Ça alors, quels grands chameaux ! Ils ont deux bosses sur le dos ! Les dromadaires que je connais n'ont qu'une seule bosse. Ruby, peux-tu leur poser des questions sur l'indice ?
Ruby : Excusez-moi, Monsieur Chameau, mes amis et moi cherchons un indice que nous devons trouver de toute urgence. Avez-vous des informations pour nous ?
M. Camel : Bonjour, jeune chien, je ne sais pas ce qu'est un indice et je suis très fatigué et je dois partir maintenant. Bonne chance !
Ruby : Oh, c'est dommage ! Merci quand même, au revoir.
Georgia : Eh bien, Ruby, qu'a-t-il dit ?
Ruby : Rien, absolument rien.
Georgia : Oh là là, cette aventure est très difficile et nous devons rentrer à la maison maintenant.
Ruby : Je suis triste Georgia, et Sam l'est aussi.

CLUE

Clue 5

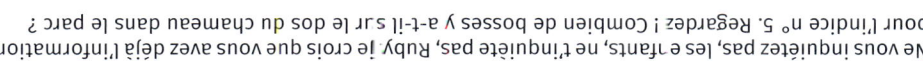

Don't worry children, don't worry Ruby, I believe you already have the information for clue number 5. Look! How many humps are there on the camel's back in the park? Write the answer in the address book at the end of this book.

Ne vous inquiétez pas, les enfants, ne t'inquiète pas, Ruby, je crois que vous avez déjà l'information pour l'indice n° 5. Regardez ! Combien de bosses y a-t-il sur le dos du chameau dans le parc ?

Look at the Animals

> **LET'S PLAY!**

LOOK AND ANSWER

❶ How many spots are there on Mrs Giraffe – six or seven?
❷ How many wolves are there in the paddock – eight or nine?
❸ Are the sheep next to the donkeys?
❹ How many penguins are in the water – two or three?
❺ How many zebras are next to the children – three or four?
❻ Is a cat chasing a chicken or a duck?

1 - 7 / 2 - 8 / 3 - yes / 4 - 2 / 5 - 3 / 6 - a chicken.

TRUE OR FALSE? (Check p. 40!)

❶ The giraffe paddock is next to the wolf paddock.
❷ There are twelve penguins.
❸ The mini farm is opposite the wolf paddock.
❹ The camels are in paddock 7.
❺ The gorillas are in the paddock next to the penguins.
❻ There are five lions in the paddock.

1T / 2F / 3T / 4F / 5F / 6F.

5 • The Wildlife Park

LET'S PLAY!

QUESTIONS ABOUT THE WILDLIFE PARK (Check p. 40!)

1. How many animals are there in paddock 3?
2. What animals are in paddock 5?
3. How many different black and white animals are there in the park today?
4. Are there any penguins in the water?
5. Are the ponies next to the donkeys in the mini farm?
6. What animals are next to the lions?

1. Eight / 2. Gorillas / 3. Three (zebras, penguins and Ruby) / 4. Yes, there are two penguins in the water. / 5. No / 6. Chimpanzees.

 DID YOU KNOW?

En anglais, on utilise souvent le même mot pour dire chameau (qui a deux bosses) et dromadaire (qui a une bosse). In English, it's a camel! Mais *dromedary* existe cependant.

Song and Recap

LET'S SING

WE'RE GOING TO THE ZOO

We're going to the zoo, zoo, zoo.
How about you, you, you?
You can come too, too, too.
We're going to the zoo, zoo, zoo.

See all the monkeys scritch, scritch scratching.
Hanging by their long tails scritch, scritch scratching.
Jumping all around and scritch, scritch scratching.
We can stay all day!

(chorus)

See the tall giraffes with long neck stretching.
Poking out tongues with long neck stretching.
Munching on leaves with long neck stretching.
We can stay all day!

(chorus)

On va aller au zoo
On va aller au zoo, zoo, zoo.
Et toi, toi, toi ?
Tu peux venir aussi, aussi, aussi.
On va au zoo, zoo, zoo.

Regardez tous les singes qui grattent, grattent, grattent.
Suspendus par leurs longues queues, grattant, grattant, grattant.
Sautant tout autour et grattant, grattant, grattant.
On peut rester toute la journée !

(Refrain)

Voir les grandes girafes avec un long cou qui s'étire.
Tirer la langue en étirant le cou.
Grignoter des feuilles avec un long cou qui s'étire.
On peut rester toute la journée !

(Refrain)

5 • The Wildlife Park

LET'S PLAY!

TRANSLATE

⭐ Relie chacune de ces expressions en anglais avec sa traduction en français.

❶ Excuse me!

❷ That's a shame!

❸ Don't worry!

Ⓐ Ne t'inquiète pas !

Ⓑ Excusez-moi !

Ⓒ C'est dommage !

1B / 2C / 3A.

Est-ce que tu connais chacun de ces mots en anglais ? Si oui, bravo, et si non, retourne au début du chapitre pour réviser et trouver le mot en anglais.

HUMP — DIFFICULT — PADDOCK — SPOT — TIRED — SAD — BIG — URGENTLY — DIFFERENT — YOUNG — WINDY — STRIPES — NOTHING — BACK — ALREADY — FARMYARD

6 The General Store

DIALOGUE

Sam: Georgia, I'm tired and hungry. Can we go and get something to eat?

Georgia: Ok Sam, me too, I'm hungry. Let's go into this shop and buy some food.

Sam: Great, and we must buy something for Ruby, too.

Georgia: Of course, you know what she likes.

Sam: Ruby, you have to wait outside. See you in a minute.

Sam : Georgia, je suis fatigué et j'ai faim. Est-ce qu'on peut aller chercher quelque chose à manger ?
Georgia : D'accord Sam, moi aussi, j'ai faim. Allons dans ce magasin et achetons quelque chose.
Sam : Super, et nous devons aussi acheter quelque chose pour Ruby.
Georgia : Bien sûr, tu sais ce qu'elle aime.
Sam : Ruby, tu dois attendre dehors. On se voit dans une minute.

6 • The General Store

COMIC STRIP

Dans la case 1, l'abeille demande : « Pourquoi es-tu triste ? »
Dans la case 2, Ruby répond : « Je suis fatiguée et j'ai faim. »
Dans la case 3, l'abeille dit : « Ne t'inquiète pas, tu vas avoir du miel. »

DIALOGUE

Shopkeeper Mr Smith: Good morning children. Can I help you?

Sam: Hello Mr Smith, yes please, I'd like a piece of shortbread.

Georgia: And can I have a chocolate muffin, please?

Mr Smith: Of course, here you are.

Sam: Do you think our friend Ruby the dog could have some honey?

Mr Smith: Honey for your dog???

Georgia: Yes, I know it's funny, but Ruby loves honey!

Mr Smith : Bonjour les enfants. Puis-je vous aider ?
Sam : Oui, s'il vous plaît, je voudrais un morceau un sablé.
Georgia : Et puis-je avoir un muffin au chocolat, s'il vous plaît ?
Mr Smith : Bien sûr, voilà.
Sam : Pensez-vous que notre ami Ruby le chien pourrait avoir un peu de miel ?
Mr Smith : Du miel pour votre chien ???
Georgia : Oui, je sais que c'est drôle, mais Ruby adore le miel !

Clue Time

VOCABULARY

COMPOUND NOUNS

 +  = cupcake

 +  = address book

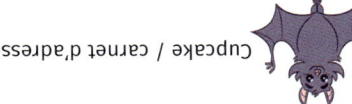
Cupcake / carnet d'adresses.

CLUE

 What does Ruby eat from the general store? Write the answer in the address book at the end of this book.
Clue 6

Quel produit du magasin mange Ruby ? Écris-le dans le carnet d'adresses qui se trouve à la fin du livre.

LET'S PLAY!

TRUE OR FALSE?

❶ The name of the shopkeeper is Mr Smith.
❷ Georgia and Sam ask for some crisps.
❸ Ruby is not hungry.
❹ A bee comes to talk to Ruby.
❺ Sam asks for a piece of shortbread.

1T / 2F / 3F / 4T / 5T.

6 • The General Store

RECIPE

How to make delicious shortbread biscuits, with help from an adult.

SHORTBREAD BISCUITS

Utensils
- A mixing bowl
- A wooden spoon, a knife and a fork
- A baking tray and a cooling rack
- A rolling pin
- Biscuit cutters

Ingredients
- 60 g of plain flour
- 20 g of caster sugar
- 40 g of butter, softened, cut into cubes

Method

1. First, wash your hands.
2. Next, ask an adult to heat the oven to 190°C.
3. Beat the butter and the sugar together.
4. Stir in the flour to make a smooth paste.
5. Place on a work surface and gently roll out with the rolling pin: the paste should be 1 cm thick.
6. Cut into rounds or fingers and place on the baking tray. Make small marks with the fork. Sprinkle with caster sugar and put in the fridge for 20 minutes.
7. Ask the adult to bake in the oven for 15-20 minutes or until golden-brown.
8. Put the shortbread to cool on the cooling rack.
9. Enjoy the delicious shortbread!

Comment préparer des biscuits sablés délicieux, avec l'aide d'un adulte (le four sera chaud !)

- 60 g de farine
- 20 g de sucre en poudre
- 40 g de beurre doux ramolli, coupé en dés

1. D'abord, se laver les mains.
2. Ensuite, demander à un adulte de préchauffer le four à 190 °C.
3. Mettre le sucre et le beurre dans un saladier et malaxer du bout des doigts pour obtenir des miettes.
4. Ajouter la farine et malaxer de nouveau.
5. Faire une grosse boule de pâte avec les mains et saupoudrer un plan de travail avec de la farine. Étaler la pâte avec le rouleau sur une épaisseur d'un centimètre.
6. Découper des ronds ou faire des rectangles. Piquer le dessus de la pâte avec une fourchette et saupoudrer de sucre. Installer sur une plaque de cuisson et faire refroidir pendant 20 minutes au réfrigérateur.
7. Demander à un adulte de faire cuire au four pendant 15 à 20 minutes, jusqu'à ce que la pâte soit légèrement dorée.
8. Laisser refroidir sur une grille.
9. Se régaler !

Activities

LET'S SING

MUFFIN MAN SONG

Do you know the muffin man, the muffin man, the muffin man?
Do you know the muffin man who lives on Drury Lane?

Yes, I know the muffin man, the muffin man, the muffin man.
Yes, I know the muffin man who lives on Drury Lane.

La chanson du vendeur de muffins
Connais-tu le vendeur de muffins ? Le vendeur de muffins.
Connais-tu le vendeur de muffins, qui vit à Drury Lane ? (chemin de Drury)
Oui ! je connais le vendeur de muffins, le vendeur de muffins.
Oui ! je connais le vendeur de muffins, qui vit à Drury Lane.

LET'S PLAY!

FILL THE GAP!

⭐ Tu es en Angleterre et tu dois acheter les ingrédients pour faire les gâteaux de la recette.

⭐ Complète les mots dans le dialogue.

You: "Hello Mr Shopk_ _ _ _ _! I would like to make some short_ _ _ _ _ biscuits. Please, can I have some s_ _ _ _, some fl_ _ _ and some bu_ _ _? Thank you very much, goodb_ _."

Shopkeeper / shortbread / sugar / flour / butter / goodbye.

6 • The General Store

LET'S PLAY!

MIXED-UP RECIPE

⭐ The shortbread recipe below is not in the right chronological order. Put the instructions in the correct order.

A Roll out with the rolling pin.

B Beat the butter and the sugar together.

C Bake in the oven for 15-20 minutes.

D Cut into rounds or fingers.

E Heat the oven to 190°C.

F Stir in the flour.

E / B / F / A / D / C

> Est-ce que tu connais chacun de ces mots en anglais ? Si oui, bravo, et si non, retourne au début du chapitre pour réviser et trouver le mot en anglais.

HAPPY • SAD • TIRED • FUNNY • HUNGRY • FOOD TO EAT

7 The Old Castle

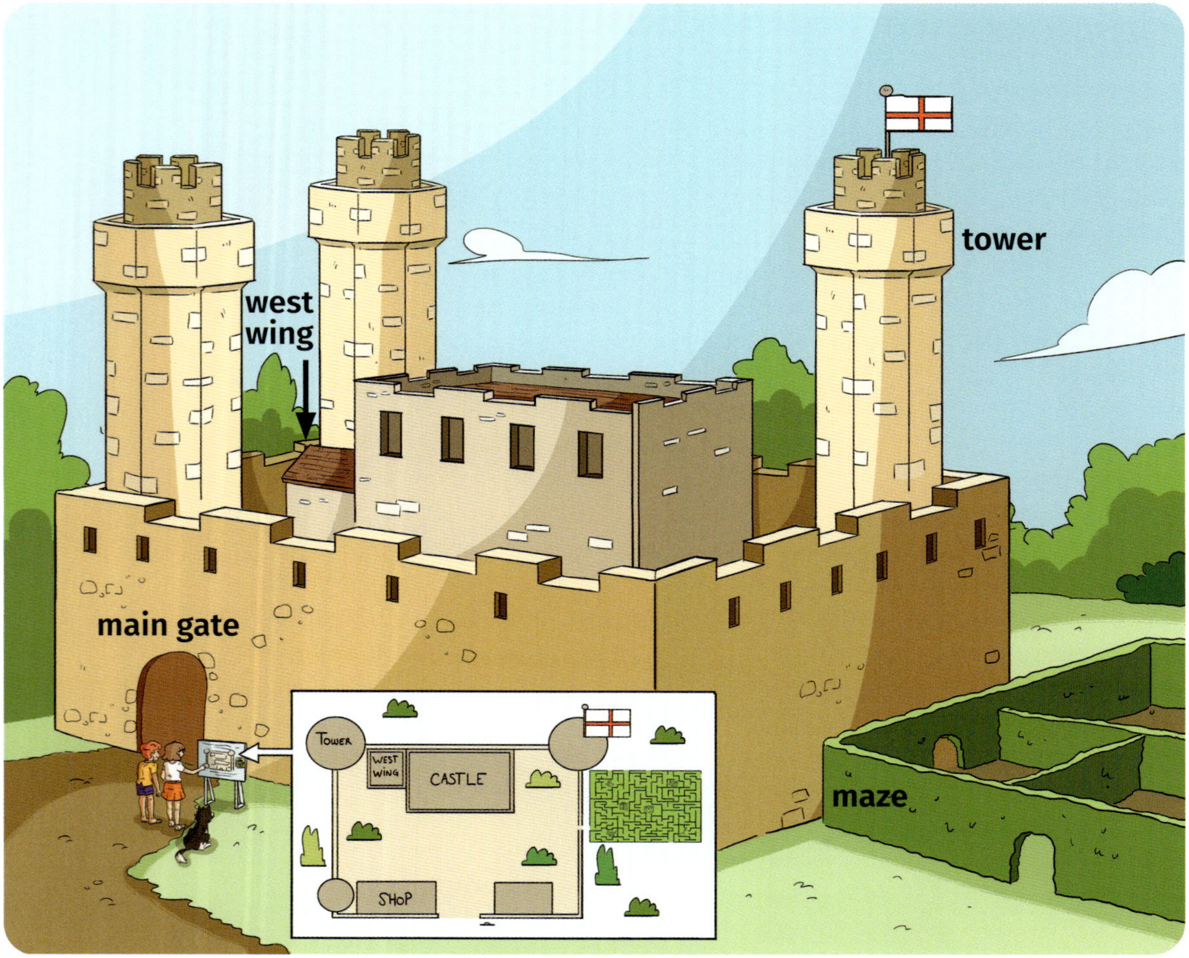

DIALOGUE

Sam: Wow, what a cool castle! Look at the gate. It's so old!

Georgia: Yes, I know, Sam, this is a medieval castle from the fifteenth century.

Sam: Where do you want to go first, Georgia? Can we go to the haunted part of the castle, please?

Georgia: No, I would like to do some archery first. We can go to the haunted part later.

7 • The Old Castle

Sam: OK, but what's happening? It's raining, and oh dear, I can hear some thunder and, wow, what a fantastic bolt of lightning!!!

Georgia: Quick, Sam, we must get out of the rain. It's raining cats and dogs now.

DIALOGUE

Rohan, the Castle Guard: Hello children, welcome to the west wing, the haunted wing of the castle.

Sam: Great stuff! We are in the haunted part of the castle.

Georgia: And we can't go to archery now as it's raining so much in this terrible storm.

Rohan: Legend says that a ghost comes when it's night and a full moon. There is a full moon tonight, so let's wait and see.

Sam: Fantastic, I hope we see something.

Georgia: Yeah, that would be awesome.

Escape from the Maze

COMIC STRIP

DIALOGUE

Georgia: Oh wow, here is a well and this is the centre of the maze. We must find our way out, before the castle closes, or we'll be here all night.

Sam: Don't worry, Georgia, I left some stones behind me as we came in. We need to turn around and follow the line of stones out of the maze.

Georgia: That's wonderful! What a clever boy you are, Sam.

Georgia : Oh là là, il y a un puits et c'est le centre du labyrinthe. Nous devons trouver la sortie avant que le château ne ferme, sinon nous y passerons la nuit.

Sam : Ne t'inquiète pas, Georgia, j'ai laissé des pierres derrière moi en entrant. Nous devons faire demi-tour et suivre la rangée de pierres pour sortir du labyrinthe.

Georgia : C'est merveilleux ! Quel garçon intelligent tu es, Sam.

7 • The Old Castle

Si tu veux te souvenir que les Anglais comparent la pluie torrentielle à des chiens qui chassent les chats, essaie d'imaginer un chien qui poursuit un chat. Le chien suit le chat, tout comme les gouttes de pluie se suivent de très près.

LET'S PLAY!

SERIES OF EVENTS

⭐ Remets les événements dans l'ordre.

❶ They all run inside the maze.

❷ Ruby decides to chase the cats.

❸ They are lost in the centre of the maze.

❹ The children follow Ruby chasing the cats.

❺ Ruby sees the cats.

5/2/4/1/3.

🇬🇧 DID YOU KNOW?

The British like to believe in ghosts and in many castles in England, Wales and Scotland, legend explains that there are haunted parts of many castles.

Les Britanniques aiment croire aux fantômes et, dans de nombreux châteaux d'Angleterre, du Pays de Galles et d'Écosse, la légende raconte qu'il existe des parties hantées.

Clue Time

LET'S PLAY!

MAZE GAME ⭐ Go to each entrance of the maze and follow the path with your finger to reach the object. Example: the word **castle** to match the image of a castle.

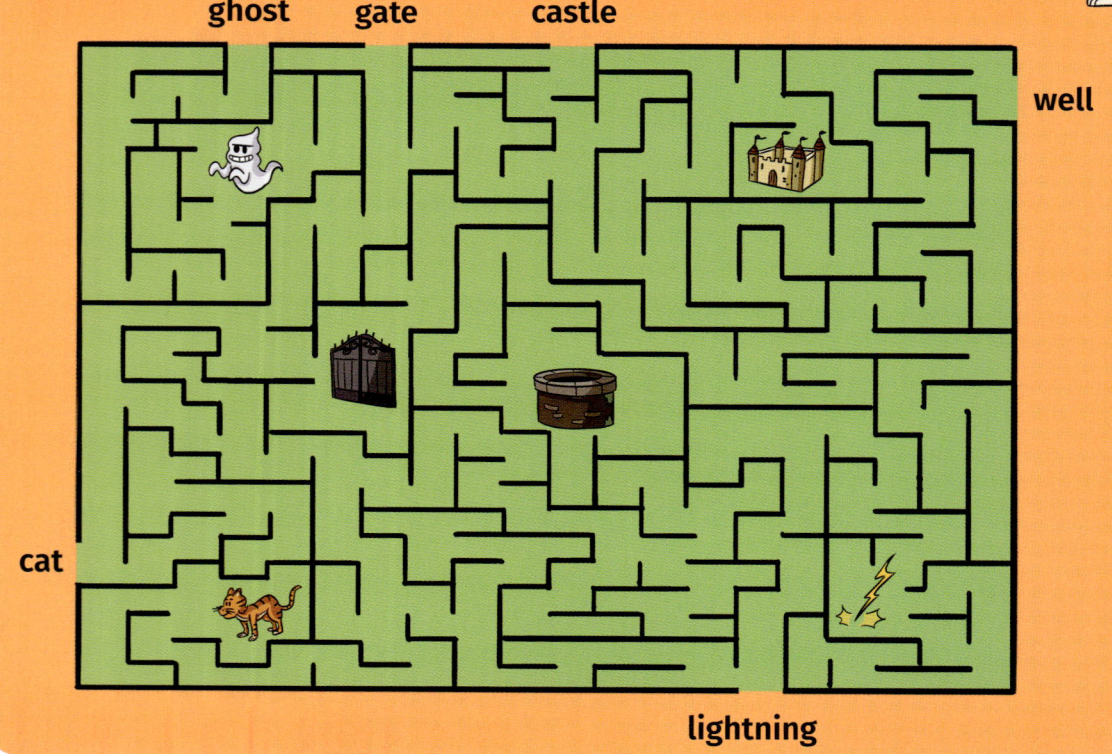

CLUE

Clue number 7 to write in the address book: what object is in the centre of the maze?

Clue 7

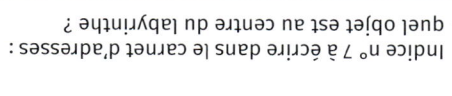
Indice n° 7 à écrire dans le carnet d'adresses : quel objet est au centre du labyrinthe ?

7 • The Old Castle

LET'S SING

IT'S RAINING, IT'S POURING

It's raining, it's pouring,
The old man is snoring.
He went to bed and
Bumped his head
And couldn't get up in the morning.

Il pleut des cordes
Il pleut des cordes,
Le vieil homme ronfle.
Il s'est couché et
S'est cogné la tête
Et n'a pas pu se lever le lendemain matin.

Est-ce que tu connais chacun de ces mots en anglais ? Si oui, bravo, et si non, retourne au début du chapitre pour réviser et trouver le mot en anglais.

THUNDER

SAFE GATE TO FOLLOW FIRST
STORM WAIT AND SEE
TONIGHT TO CLOSE
WELL OLD
HAUNTED
WING NIGHT
CLEVER
MEDIEVAL MAZE
WONDERFUL

8 The Funfair

big wheel
roller coaster
dodgems
Joe's Dodgem Cars
hoopla stall
HOOPLA
CAROUSEL
LONDON BUS TOUR
carousel
hot dog and burger stand
AMUSEMENT PARK
TICKET OFFICE

DIALOGUE

Georgia: Look Sam, an amusement park!

Sam: Wow, look at the rides! There's a roller coaster and I can see the dodgems!

Georgia: Sam, give Ruby the map. She wants to talk.

Ruby: This looks very dangerous! Look how fast the dodgem cars go! Look how high the rollercoaster is! You must be very careful.

8 • The Funfair

Georgia: Don't be scared, Ruby, it isn't dangerous. We need to find clue number 8 for the address book. We will be quick.

Sam: Let's buy a bag of tokens at the ticket office. Hello, can we have a bag of tokens, please?

The Ticket lady: Yes, here you are. That's five pounds, please. Have fun!

Georgia : Regarde, Sam ! Un parc d'attractions !
Sam : Wow, regarde les jeux ! Il y a une montagne russe et je peux voir les voitures auto-tamponneuses !
Georgia : Sam, donne la carte à Ruby. Elle veut parler.
Ruby : Cela a l'air très dangereux ! Regardez la vitesse des voitures auto-tamponneuses. Regardez la hauteur de la montagne russe ! Vous devez faire très attention.
Georgia : N'aie pas peur, Ruby, ce n'est pas dangereux. Nous devons trouver l'indice numéro 8 pour remplir le carnet d'adresses. Nous ferons vite.
Sam : Achetons un sac de jetons au guichet. Bonjour Madame, pouvons-nous avoir un sac de jetons s'il vous plaît ?
La dame de l'entrée : Oui, voici. Cela fait 5 livres, s'il vous plaît. Amusez-vous bien !

COMIC STRIP

Dans la case 2, Ruby dit : « Grrrr ! Va-t-en ! »

🇬🇧 DID YOU KNOW?

Hull Fair is Europe's largest travelling funfair. It has been held since 1278, when King Edward I authorised it by Royal Charter. Hull Fair is held every year around 11th October and lasts for one week.

Hull Fair est la plus importante fête foraine itinérante d'Europe. Elle a lieu chaque année : le Roi Edouard 1er l'a autorisée par Charte Royale en 1278. Hull Fair est toujours organisée autour du 11 octobre et dure une semaine.

Joe's Dodgems

a dodgem
a driver

Hello, I'm Joe. These are my dodgem cars.

DIALOGUE

Georgia: Look Sam, look Ruby! Dodgems! Let's have a ride. We can pay with our tokens! Sam, you can drive but Ruby, you can't drive. You must wait here.

Joe: Hello, children, would you like a go on my dodgems? Can you drive? I'm sorry, but your dog can't drive the dodgems.

Georgia: Hello Joe, we would love a ride. Sam and I can drive.

Joe: That's two tokens, please. You can each choose a car and start to drive.

Sam: Can I have the yellow car please, Joe?

Georgia: Can I have the blue car please?

Joe: Yes, you can. Have fun but be careful!

Georgia : Regarde, Sam, regarde, Ruby ! Les autos-tamponneuses ! Faisons un tour ! Nous pouvons payer avec nos jetons ! Sam, tu sais conduire, mais Ruby, tu ne sais pas conduire. Tu dois attendre ici.

Joe : Bonjour les enfants, voulez-vous faire un tour d'autos-tamponneuses ? Savez-vous conduire ? Je suis désolé, mais votre chien ne peut pas conduire les autos-tamponneuses.

Georgia : Bonjour Joe, on voudrait faire un tour. Sam et moi savons conduire.

Joe : Ça fera deux jetons, s'il vous plaît. Vous pouvez choisir une voiture chacun et commencer à conduire.

Sam : Est-ce que je peux prendre la voiture jaune, s'il vous plaît, Joe ?

Georgia : Est-ce que je peux prendre la voiture bleue, s'il vous plaît ?

Joe : Oui, vous pouvez. Amusez-vous mais faites attention !

8 • The Funfair

DIALOGUE

Sam: Look out Georgia! Be careful! The red car is coming towards you! Help!

Georgia: Whew! Let's get out now.

Sam: I'm tired and hungry, Georgia.

Georgia: Me too, Sam. Oh, look! A hotdog stand! Let's eat a hotdog! Yum! I'm hungry!

Sam: Don't worry, Ruby! A hotdog is a sandwich with a frankfurter sausage, not a real dog!

Sam : Regarde, Georgia ! Fais attention ! La voiture rouge fonce sur toi ! Au secours !
Georgia : Eh bien ! Sortons maintenant.
Sam : Je suis fatigué et j'ai faim, Georgia.
Georgia : Moi aussi, Sam. Oh, regarde ! Une buvette ! Mangeons un hotdog ! J'ai faim !
Sam : Ne t'inquiète pas, Ruby ! Un hotdog est un sandwich avec une saucisse de Francfort, pas un vrai chien !

Clue Time

DIALOGUE

Georgia: Look Sam, a carousel! There is a unicorn! And an aeroplane!

Sam: And a fire engine! And a sports car! And a London bus! Can we have a ride?

Georgia: No, Sam, Ruby says no. We must find Clue 8 now.

Georgia : Regarde, Sam ! Un manège ! Il y a une licorne ! Et un avion !
Sam : Et un camion des pompiers ! Et une voiture de sport ! Et un bus Londonien ! Est-ce que nous pouvons faire un tour ?
Georgia : Non, Sam, Ruby dit non. Il faut trouver l'indice numéro 8 maintenant.

LET'S PLAY!

TRUE OR FALSE?

❶ The lady gives tokens to Sam.
❷ The children eat a burger.
❸ Georgia is hungry.
❹ A hotdog is a real dog.
❺ Georgia is driving a yellow car.
❻ Sam is driving a blue car.
❼ Ruby isn't driving a car.
❽ The man who operates the dodgems is called Joe.

1T / 2F / 3T / 4F / 5F / 6F / 7T / 8T.

8 • The Funfair

CLUE

You must find clue number 8 for the address book. What can Sam and Georgia do on the dodgem cars, but Ruby can't?
D _ _ _ _

Clue 8

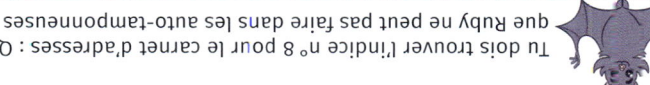

Tu dois trouver l'indice n° 8 pour le carnet d'adresses : Qu'est-ce que Ruby ne peut pas faire dans les auto-tamponneuses ?

LET'S PLAY!

WORDSEARCH ★ Words to find: dodgems / drive / hotdog / hoopla / token / sausage.

K	D	Z	D	O	D	G	E	M	S	K
R	R	A	N	V	C	F	N	C	M	Y
T	I	B	N	F	D	K	B	Q	B	T
O	V	Z	V	H	O	T	D	O	G	M
L	E	F	T	J	H	V	X	K	D	Y
K	W	Q	T	O	K	E	N	B	O	K
Y	T	N	D	M	J	V	Z	R	D	M
N	L	M	S	A	U	S	A	G	E	Z
R	R	D	U	I	F	D	Y	E	U	X
H	O	O	P	L	A	N	D	F	K	M

Attractions

LET'S SING

DODGEM SONG

Let's go riding in a dodgem
The dodgems that you find at the fair
Let's go riding in a dodgem
You're not supposed to bump them so drive with care

Let's go riding in a dodgem
The dodgems that you find at the fair
Let's go riding in a dodgem
You're not supposed to bump them so drive with care

You've got to dodgem, dodgem, dodgem, dodgem
Let's go 'round the other way
You've got to dodgem, dodgem, dodgem, dodgem
I could ride a dodgem all day

La chanson de auto-tamponneuse

Allons faire un tour dans une auto-tamponneuse
Les auto-tamponneuses que tu trouves à la foire
Allons faire un tour dans une auto-tamponneuse
Tu ne dois pas les heurter donc conduis prudemment

Allons faire un tour dans une auto-tamponneuse
Les auto-tamponneuses que tu trouves à la foire
Allons faire un tour dans une auto-tamponneuse
Tu ne dois pas les heurter donc conduis prudemment

Il faut les esquiver, esquiver, esquiver
Tournons dans l'autre sens
Il faut les esquiver, esquiver, esquiver
Je pourrais passer toute la journée dans une auto-tamponneuse

8 • The Funfair

🇬🇧 DID YOU KNOW?

The London Eye is a 135-metre-high big wheel. It is also called "the Millenium Wheel" as it first opened on 31st December 1999. Located in the heart of London, it has three million visitors a year.

Le London Eye est une grande roue de 135 mètres de haut. Elle est également appelée « roue du millénaire », car elle a été inaugurée le 31 décembre 1999. Située au cœur de Londres, elle accueille trois millions de visiteurs chaque année.

Est-ce que tu connais chacun de ces mots en anglais ? Si oui, bravo, et si non, retourne au début du chapitre pour réviser et trouver le mot en anglais.

TICKET OFFICE
ROLLER COASTER
BE CAREFUL!
DODGEMS

9 The Beach

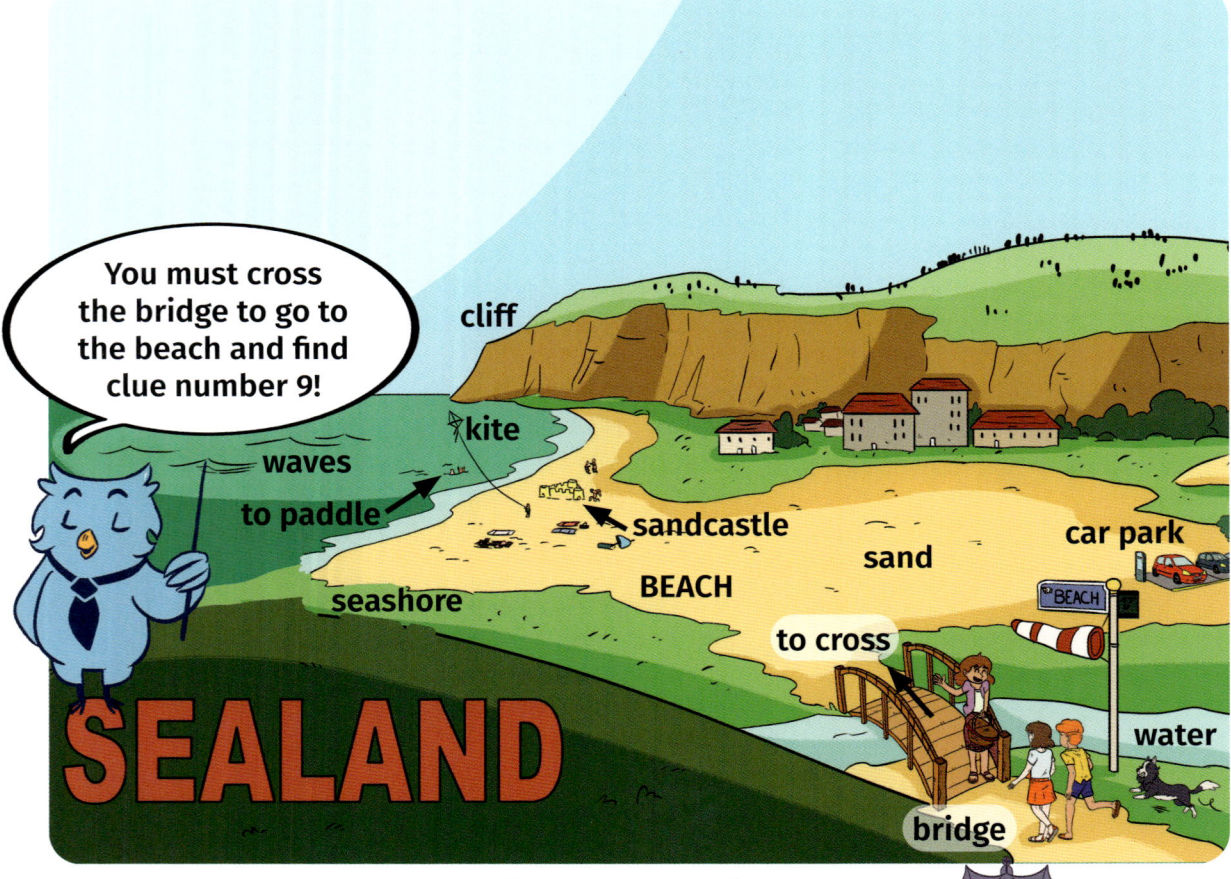

Tu dois traverser le pont pour aller à la plage et trouver l'indice n° 9.

DIALOGUE

Georgia: Mum, can we go on the beach?

Mum: Yes, let's go on the beach. We must cross the bridge to go to the car park and the beach.

Georgia: Ooh mum, look at the sea! It's beautiful! The waves are quite big. Can we paddle?

Mum: Yes, you can paddle but you can't swim because it's dangerous. The waves are too big. It's very windy: look how high that kite is flying!

9 • The Beach

Ruby: Be quick! The sea is very dangerous and we must find clue number 9!

Georgia: Come on, Sam, let's go and paddle in the waves. Look, Ruby is afraid of the waves!

Georgia : Maman, est-ce que nous pouvons aller sur la plage ?
Mum : Oui, allons-y. Nous devons traverser le pont pour accéder au parking et à la plage.
Georgia : Oh ! Maman, regarde la mer ! C'est beau ! Les vagues sont plutôt grosses. Est-ce que nous pouvons y barboter ?
Mum : Oui, vous pouvez barboter, mais vous ne pouvez pas nager parce que c'est dangereux. Les vagues sont trop grosses. Il y a beaucoup de vent : regardez comme le cerf-volant vole haut !
Ruby : Dépêchez-vous ! La mer est très dangereuse et nous devons trouver l'indice numéro 9 !
Georgia : Viens, Sam, allons barboter dans les vagues. Regarde, Ruby a peur de vagues !

VOCABULARY

windy

cloudy

stormy

 **DID YOU KNOW?**

The strongest winds ever recorded in the UK have been on mountains, and the strongest gust was 150.3 knots (173 mph) recorded at Cairngorm Summit on 20 March 1986. Note that 173 mph (miles per hour) = 278 km/hour.

Les vents les plus forts jamais enregistrés au Royaume-Uni l'ont été sur des montagnes, et la rafale la plus forte jamais enregistrée a été de 150,3 nœuds (173 mph) au sommet de Cairngorm, le 20 mars 1986. Notons que 173 mph (miles par heure) = 278 km/h.

LET'S PLAY!

TRUE OR FALSE?

❶ Georgia and Sam are going to the beach with Georgia's mum.

❷ Georgia wants to paddle in the sea.

❸ Ruby isn't afraid of the waves.

1T / 2T / 3F.

Let's Have a Picnic!

DIALOGUE

Mum: Come on, Georgia! Come on, Sam! Come and sit down on the picnic blanket and have lunch. Here are some delicious egg and ham sandwiches. There is some fruit juice or water, if you're thirsty. Here is some food for Ruby.

Sam: Thank you very much!

Georgia: Look, Mum! Look Sam! There's an ice cream van. I love ice creams, don't you, Sam? Mum, can we have an ice cream for dessert, please?

Mum: Yes, you can, but be quick. We must go home soon.

Mum : Viens, Georgia ! Viens, Sam ! Venez vous asseoir sur la couverture pour déjeuner. Voici de délicieux sandwiches aux œufs et au jambon. Il y a des jus de fruits ou de l'eau si vous avez soif. Voici de la nourriture pour Ruby.

Sam : Merci beaucoup !

Georgia : Regarde, Maman ! Regarde Sam ! Il y a une camionnette qui vend des glaces. J'aime beaucoup les glaces, et toi, Sam ? Maman, est-ce que nous pouvons avoir une glace pour le dessert, s'il te plaît ?

Mum : Oui, mais dépêchez-vous. Nous devons rentrer à la maison bientôt.

9 • The Beach

DIALOGUE

Poppy: Hello, children! Would you prefer a popsicle or an ice cream cornet?

Georgia: Sam would like a raspberry popsicle, and I would prefer a strawberry ice cream cornet, please.

Poppy: Here is the popsicle for Sam, the ice cream for you and a biscuit for your dog.

Georgia and Sam: Thank you very much!

Mum: Let's go home now!

Poppy : Bonjour les enfants. Préférez-vous un bâtonnet ou un cornet de glace ?
Georgia : Sam aimerait un bâtonnet à la framboise et je préférerais un cornet de glace à la fraise, s'il vous plaît.
Poppy : Voici le bâtonnet pour Sam, la glace pour toi et un biscuit pour votre chien.
Georgia and Sam : Merci beaucoup !
Mum : Rentrons à la maison, maintenant.

Clue Time

VOCABULARY

COMPOUND NOUNS

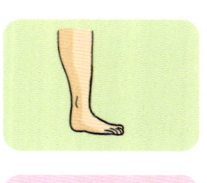 +  = football

 + 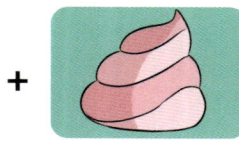 = ice cream

Voici encore des mots composés de deux mots.

LET'S PLAY!

Now it's your turn. Try to find the missing words.

MISSING WORDS

❶ Georgia and Sam are making a  +  =

❷ Georgia's mum is carrying a  +  =

❸ Georgia would like a  + =

1. Sandcastle / 2. Picnic basket / 3. Strawberry ice cream.

9 • The Beach

CLUE

The answer to the riddle will give you clue number 9. Write it in the address book. I'm made of wood. Georgia's mum, Georgia, Sam and Ruby walk across me to go to the beach. What am I?
I am a B - - - E

La réponse à l'énigme te donnera l'indice n° 9. Écris-le dans le carnet d'adresses. « Je suis fait de bois. La mère de Georgia, Georgia, Sam et Ruby m'ont traversé pour aller à la plage. Qui suis-je ? »

LET'S PLAY!

WORDSEARCH ⭐ Words to find: bridge / ham / ice cream / egg / sandwich / popsicle.

P	O	P	S	I	C	L	E	K	B
E	K	J	I	R	Z	H	O	Y	R
T	G	L	C	Z	A	K	B	C	I
S	A	N	D	W	I	C	H	P	D
U	Z	F	R	W	R	N	Z	L	G
I	C	E	C	R	E	A	M	I	E
T	Y	U	M	A	P	E	X	N	V
Q	E	F	E	G	G	D	C	R	S
H	A	M	V	X	J	I	O	B	K

73

By the Sea

LET'S SING

A SAILOR WENT TO SEA, SEA, SEA

⭐ Si tu regardes cette vidéo, tu verras deux filles qui chantent la chanson avec les gestes. Essaie de faire comme elles !

A sailor went to sea, sea, sea
To see what he could see, see, see
But all that he could see, see, see
Was the bottom of the deep blue sea, sea, sea!

A sailor went to chop, chop, chop
To see what he could chop, chop, chop
But all that he could chop, chop, chop
Was the bottom of the deep blue chop, chop, chop!

A sailor went to knee, knee, knee
To see what he could knee, knee, knee
But all that he could knee, knee, knee
Was the bottom of the deep blue knee, knee, knee!

A sailor went to sea, chop, knee
To see what he could see, chop, knee
But all that he could see, chop, knee
Was the bottom of the deep blue sea, chop, knee!

Un marin est allé en mer, mer
Un marin est allé en mer, mer, mer
Pour voir ce qu'il pouvait voir, voir, voir
Mais tout ce qu'il pouvait voir, voir, voir
C'était le fond de la mer si bleue, bleue, bleue !

Un marin est allé à coupe, coupe, coupe
Pour voir ce qu'il pouvait coupe, coupe, coupe
Mais tout ce qu'il pouvait coupe, coupe, coupe
C'était le fond de la coupe, coupe, coupe !

Un marin est allé à genou, genou, genou
Pour voir ce qu'il pouvait genou, genou, genou
Mais tout ce qu'il pouvait genou, genou, genou
C'était le fond du genou, genou, genou !

Un marin est allé en mer, coupe, genou
Pour voir ce qu'il pouvait voir, coupe, genou
Mais tout ce qu'il pouvait voir, coupe, genou
C'était le fond de la mer si bleue, coupe, genou !

74

9 • The Beach

TONGUE TWISTERS

Essaie de dire cette phrase le plus rapidement possible, sans te tordre la langue : « She sells seashells on the seashore. »

This is a shell.

This is the seashore.

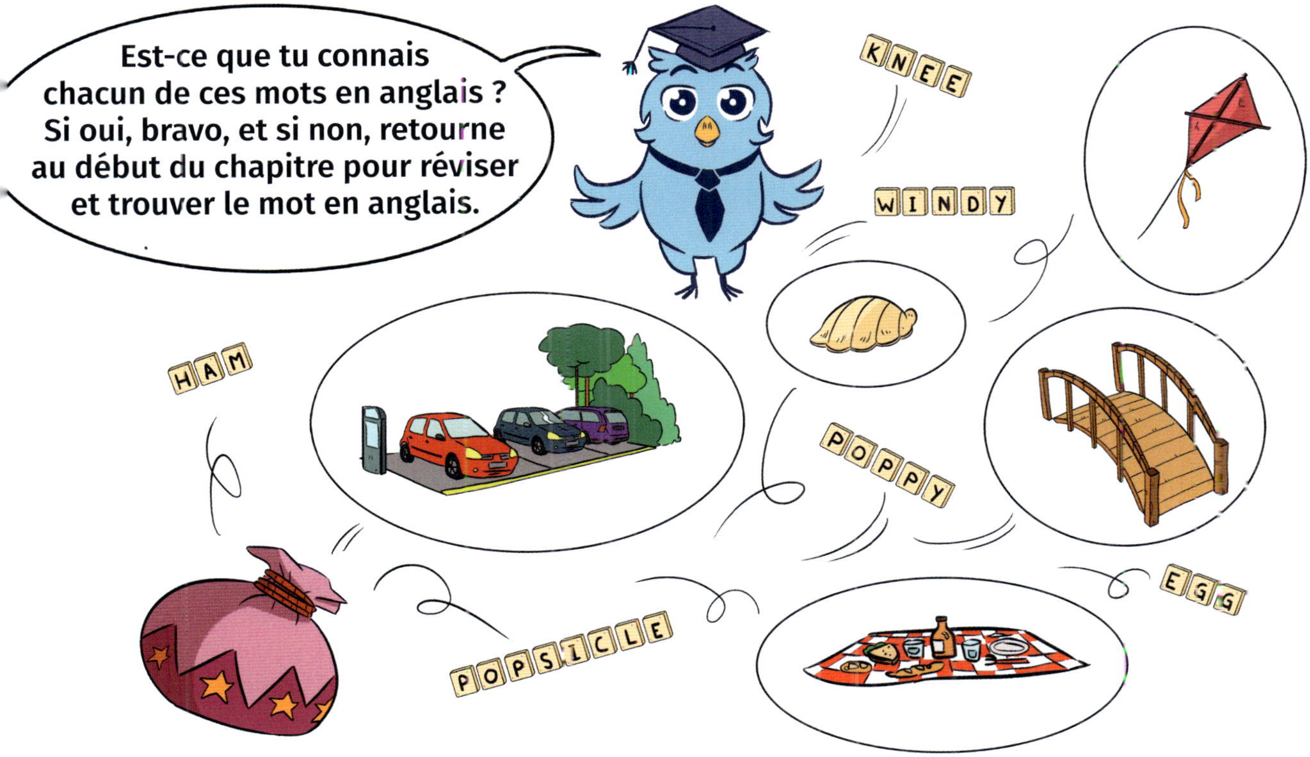

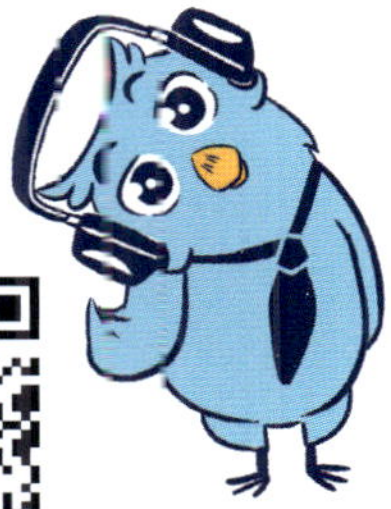

Est-ce que tu connais chacun de ces mots en anglais ? Si oui, bravo, et si non, retourne au début du chapitre pour réviser et trouver le mot en anglais.

10 Activity Centre

DIALOGUE

Georgia: The children are having fun! There are lots of children doing sport and playing games. Let's ask that man if we can go into the activity centre to look for the clue.

Matt: Hello, children, and hello, dog! I'm Matt, the sports trainer. Are you coming to participate in our sports activities and our games? We are playing football and basketball, and the younger children are playing hopscotch.

10 • Activity Centre

Georgia: Hello Matt. No, thank you, we don't have time because we are on a quest for clues to help our friend Ruby find her family.

Matt: What are you looking for in this school? Can I help you?

Sam: We are looking for a clue so that we can discover the new address of Ruby's family.

Matt: Wow! Good luck! You can go inside the school to meet Olivia, the teacher.

Georgia: Thank you, Matt. Come on Sam and Ruby, let's go inside the school.

Georgia : Les enfants sont en train de s'amuser ! Il y a beaucoup d'enfants qui sont en train de faire du sport et de jouer. Demandons à cet homme si nous pouvons entrer dans le centre aéré pour chercher l'indice.

Matt : Bonjour, les enfants, et bonjour, le chien. Je m'appelle Matt et je suis le coach sportif. Est-ce vous venez participer à nos activités sportives et nos jeux ? Nous sommes en train de jouer au foot et au basket, et les plus jeunes enfants jouent à la marelle.

Georgia : Bonjour Matt. Non, merci, nous n'avons pas le temps parce que nous sommes en quête des indices pour aider notre amie Ruby à retrouver sa famille.

Matt : Que cherchez-vous dans cette école ? Est-ce que je peux vous aider ?

Sam : Nous cherchons un indice pour nous aider à découvrir la nouvelle adresse de la famille de Ruby.

Matt : Waouh ! Bonne chance ! Vous pouvez rentrer dans l'école pour rencontrer Olivia, la maîtresse.

Georgia : Merci, Matt. Venez, Sam et Ruby. Entrons dans l'école.

COMIC STRIP

 ## DID YOU KNOW?

En Grande-Bretagne, comme en France, on utilise les écoles comme des centres aérés pour accueillir les enfants pendant les vacances scolaires. On les appelle « Holiday Activity Centres ».

In the Classroom

COMIC STRIP

DIALOGUE

The children: Ooh, look, a dog!

Olivia: Come in! Hello, children, and hello, dog. Welcome to the activity centre. My name is Olivia and I am a teacher. The children are studying the map of our town. What are your names?

10 • Activity Centre

Georgia: I'm Georgia and this is Sam and this is our friend Ruby.

Olivia: Nice to meet you. Can I help you?

Georgia: Yes, please. We are on a quest for clues to help our friend Ruby find her family.

Olivia: Oh dear! Is Ruby lost?

Georgia: Yes, she is. But we are looking everywhere for clues to find her family's new address.

Olivia: You are welcome to visit the classrooms. I hope you find your clue. Now, children, we are going to sing your favourite song, "Ruby Lou".

The children: Hooray!

Georgia: Thank you very much, Olivia.

Les enfants : Oh, regardez ! Un chien !

Olivia : Entrez ! Bonjour, les enfants, et bonjour, le chien. Soyez les bienvenus au centre aéré. Je m'appelle Olivia et je suis la maîtresse. Les enfants sont en train d'étudier une carte de notre ville. Comment vous appelez-vous ?

Georgia : Je m'appelle Georgia et voici Sam et notre amie Ruby.

Olivia : Je suis heureuse de vous rencontrer. Pu s-je vous aider ?

Georgia : Oui, s'il vous plaît. Nous sommes en quête d'indices pour aider notre amie Ruby à retrouver sa famille.

Olivia : O l là ! Est-ce que Ruby est perdue ?

Georgia : Oui, elle est perdue. Mais nous sommes en train de chercher parto_t les indices pour trouver la nouvelle adresse de sa famille.

Olivia : Je vous laisse découvrir les salles de cours. J'espère que vous allez trouver votre indice. Maintenant, les enfants, nous allons chanter votre chanson favorite, « Ruby Lou ».

Les enfants : Hourrah !

Georgia : Merci beaucoup, Olivia.

GRAMMAR

> En anglais, on décrit une activité qui est en train de se passer en utilisant le présent continu (« present continuous »).

PRESENT CONTINUOUS

Exemples :

« I am **sing**ing. » (Je suis en train de chanter.)

« The children are **play**ing. » (Les enfants sont en train de jouer.)

Et il y a aussi plein de mots de vocabulaire anglais pour décrire des activités qui se terminent en « ing ».

Exemples : **sing**ing (le chant), **writ**ing (l'écriture), **run**ning (la course à pied), **swim**ming (la natation), **read**ing (la lecture), **jump**ing (le saut)… et tant d'autres. Pratique !

The Map on the Wall

LET'S SING

RUBY LOU SONG

⭐ Le titre d'origine de la chanson est « Here we go Looby Loo » mais, par magie, nous l'avons changé pour Ruby.

Here we go Ruby Lou
Here we go Ruby Light
Here we go Ruby Lou
To the left and to the right.

You put your right foot in
You take your right foot out
You give your right leg a shake, shake, shake
And kick the ball about.

Here we go Ruby Lou
Here we go Ruby Light
Here we go Ruby Lou
To the left and to the right.

You put your left foot in
You take your left foot out
You give your left leg a shake, shake, shake
And kick the ball about.

La chanson de Ruby Lou

On y va, Ruby Lou,
On y va, Ruby Light,
On y va, Ruby Lou
Vers la gauche et vers la droite.
Avance ta jambe droite
Retire ta jambe droite
Secoue ta jambe droite
Et tape dans le ballon.

On y va, Ruby Lou,
On y va, Ruby Light,
On y va, Ruby Lou
Vers la gauche et vers la droite.
Avance ta jambe gauche
Retire ta jambe gauche
Secoue ta jambe gauche
Et tape dans le ballon.

10 • Activity Centre

DIALOGUE

Georgia: Let's have a look around the classroom.

Sam: There are lots of posters on the walls.

Georgia: Sam, take the map and give it to Ruby. Ruby wants to talk.

Ruby: Look! There is a map on the wall! Is it the town map?

Georgia: Wow! Yes, it's called "Town Map". It looks like Ruby's magic map! I hope this helps us find clue number 10!

Georgia : Regardons dans la salle de cours.
Sam : Il y a beaucoup de posters aux murs.
Georgia : Sam, sors la carte et donne-la à Ruby. Ruby veut parler.
Ruby : Regardez ! Il y a une carte affichée au mur ! Est-ce que c'est la carte de la ville ?
Georgia : Waouh ! Oui, elle s'intitule « *Town Map* ». La carte ressemble à la Ruby's Magic Map! J'espère que cela va nous aider à trouver l'indice numéro 10 !

VOCABULARY

COMPOUND NOUNS

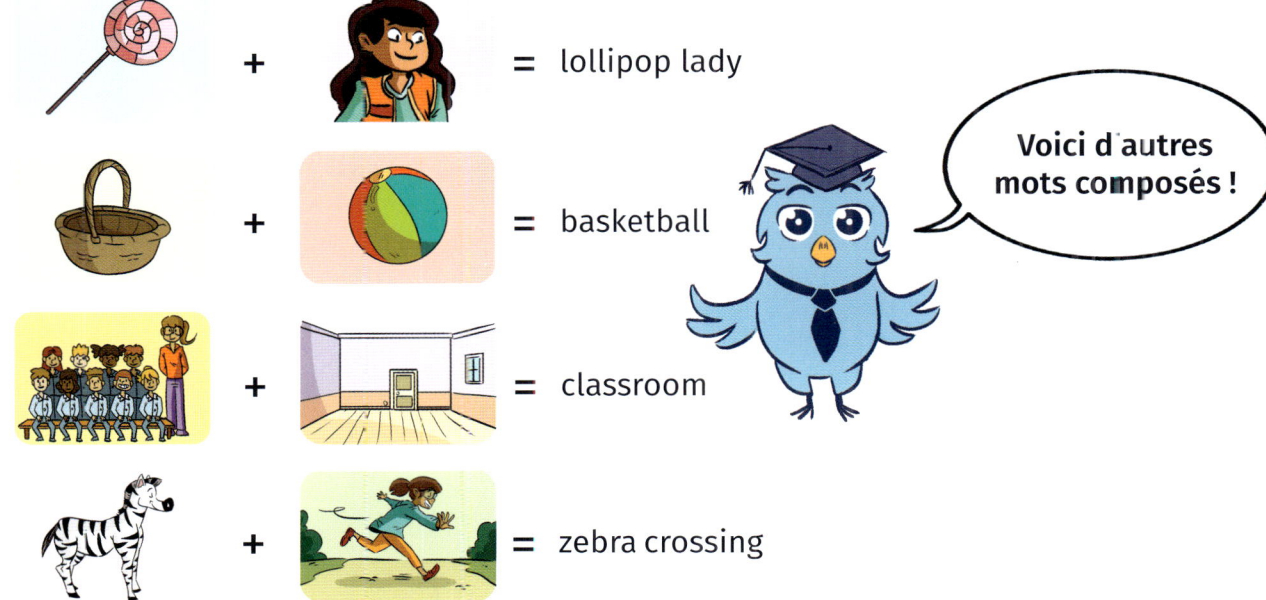

Voici d'autres mots composés !

= lollipop lady

= basketball

= classroom

= zebra crossing

81

Clue Time

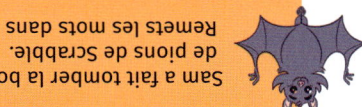

LET'S PLAY!

WORD SCRAMBLE ★ Sam has dropped the box of Scrabble letters. Please put the words into the correct order.

Sam a fait tomber la boîte de pions de Scrabble. Remets les mots dans l'ordre.

1. L L S K A B T A E B
2. T F O L A O B
3. K C O C L
4. N O T W   P A M
5. C T O H C O H P S

1. Basketball / 2. Football / 3. Clock / 4. Town Map / 5. Hopscotch.

 **DID YOU KNOW?**

British children go to school every day of the week, Monday to Friday. The school day starts at 9 in the morning and finishes at 3.30 in the afternoon. Most children wear school uniform.

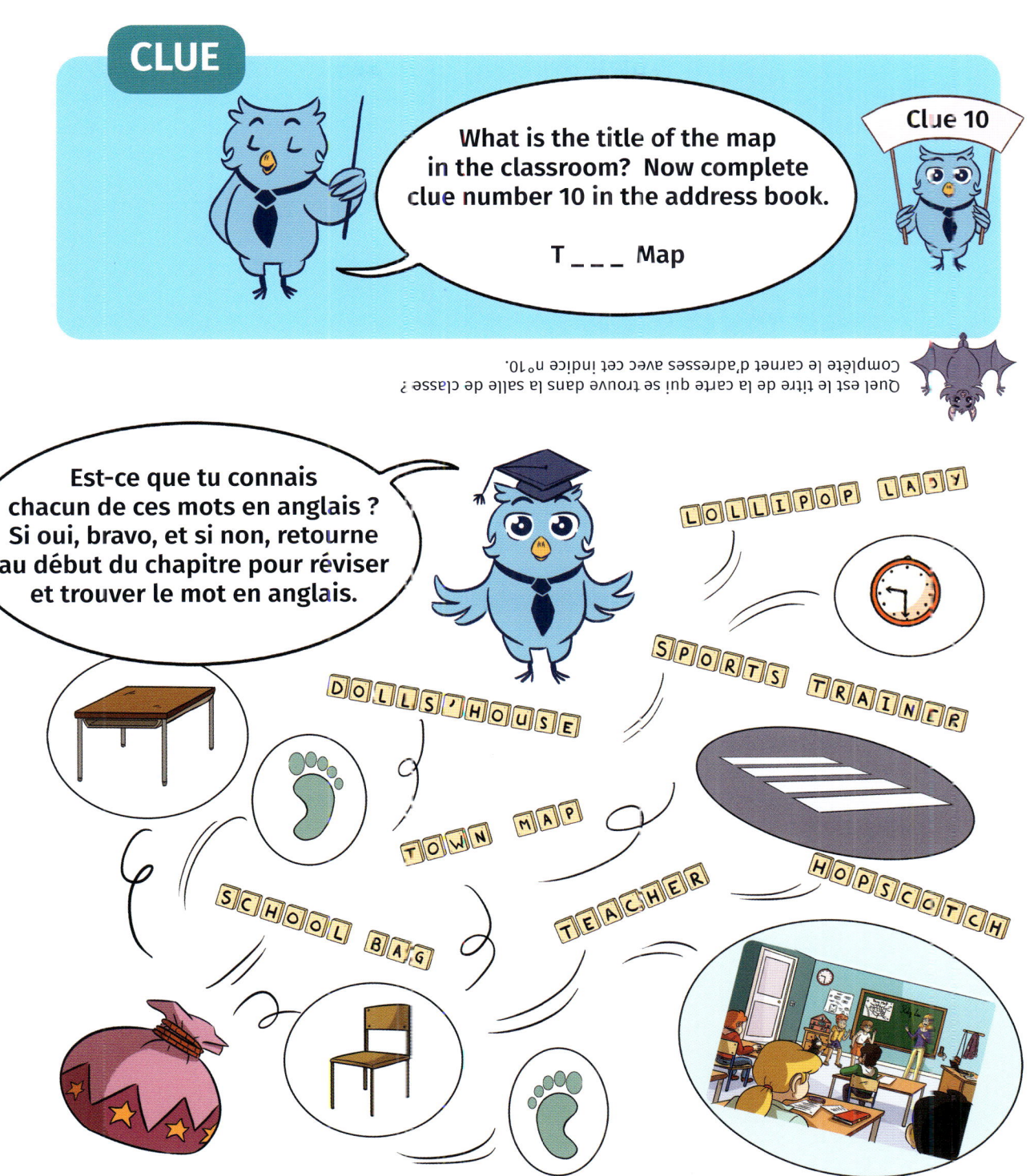

On révise ?

COMPOUND NOUNS

⭐ Match one word on the left to the correct word on the right to make a compound noun.

sweet	buttons
address	room
jelly	money
goody	bag
ticket	fair
pocket	shop
fruit	babies
chocolate	pastilles
bed	book
fun	office

Sweetshop / address book / jelly babies / goody bag / ticket office / pocket money / fruit pastilles / chocolate buttons / bedroom / funfair.

On révise ?

THE CORRECT DESCRIPTION

⭐ Match the words on the left to the clue on the right.

① I am a dodgem car.   Ⓐ You cross over me to get to the beach.
② I am a hotdog.   Ⓑ You can drive me.
③ I am Guide Owl.   Ⓒ You write addresses here.
④ I am a bridge.   Ⓓ You can eat me.
⑤ I am an address book.   Ⓔ I am a blue bird and I help you in this book.

1E / 2D / 3E / 4A / 5C.

THERE IS / ARE

⭐ Choose "there is" or "there are" to complete the sentence correctly.

There are/there is…. two cats in the story "Ruby's Magic Map".

There is/there are… one old castle in this book.

There is/there are… seven colours in a rainbow.

There is/there are… many songs in this book.

There is/there are… a number 11 on the football shirt which Sam buys.

There are two cats. / There is one castle. / There are seven colours. / There are many songs. / There is a number 11.

On révise ?

WHO AM I?

⭐ Read the description and decide who is speaking.

❶ I have glasses. My hair is brown. I live in a house called a cottage. We visit my mum in Scene 3. Who am I?

❷ I am yellow and I am a bird. I hold a microphone and I invite you to listen to the songs in the book. Who am I?

❸ I work in a funfair. I am in charge of the dodgem cars. My hair is blond. I say to Ruby that she can't ride the dodgem cars because she's a dog. Who am I?

❹ I am an animal. I am grey. I live in the wildlife park and I help Ruby. Sometimes, people think animals like me are ferocious, but in this book, I am kind. Who am I?

❺ I work in a toyshop. I invite Georgia, Sam and Ruby into my shop. I sell a football shirt to Sam. Who am I?

❻ I am a castle guard. I work in an old castle, which is haunted. I tell Georgia and Sam to go the west wing of the old castle. Who am I?

Who am I?

1. Georgia / 2. Coco the Canary / 3. Joe / 4. Nikko the wolf / 5. William / 6. Rohan.

On révise ?

PLACE AND MOVEMENT

★ For each of the prepositions in the following sentences, choose from these words: **in front of** / **in** / **on** / **between** / **outside** / **above** / **towards**.

❶ Georgia habite **dans** une maison que les Britanniques appellent « a cottage ».

❷ La maman de Georgia pose les sandwiches pour le pique-nique **sur** la couverture.

❸ Au secours ! Le méchant voyou vient **vers** moi dans la voiture auto-tamponneuse !

❹ L'arc en ciel est **au-dessus** de nos têtes.

❺ Le hotdog est un sandwich de pain avec une saucisse **entre** les deux morceaux de pain.

❻ Sur le panneau **devant** le stand des auto-tamponneuses, il est écrit « Can you drive? »

❼ Ruby doit attendre **hors** du magasin.

1. in / 2. on / 3. towards / 4. above / 5. between / 6. in front of / 7. outside.

On révise ?

CHRONOLOGICAL ORDER

⭐ Put the events in chronological order:

Scene 5: The Wildlife Park

① Ruby asks the camel about the clue.

② Ruby meets Nikko the Wolf.

③ The giraffe helps the children.

④ Georgia and Sam look at the gorillas.

⑤ Lou tells Nikko the Wolf about the clue.

Scene 7: The Old Castle

① The children and Ruby go into the maze.

② Rohan, the castle guard, tells the children and Ruby to go to the west wing.

③ It's raining a lot and there is a storm.

④ Sam left some stones behind him.

⑤ Sam wants to see a ghost.

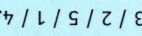

On révise ?

Scene 8: The Funfair

① Joe says to Georgia and Sam that they can drive the dodgem cars.

② Georgia, Sam and Ruby arrive in front of the ticket office.

③ Georgia and Sam eat a hotdog.

④ Ruby says "no".

⑤ Georgia and Sam buy tickets.

2 / 5 / 1 / 3 / 4.

Scene 9: The Beach

① Georgia and Sam paddle in the sea.

② They cross the bridge.

③ The children eat an ice cream and a popsicle.

④ Georgia's mum prepares the picnic.

⑤ Ruby says "Be quick! The sea is very dangerous and we must find Clue 9".

2 / 5 / 1 / 4 / 3.

WEATHER WORDS AND COLOURS

★ Choose from these words to complete the sentences: **rainy / purple / thunder / sunny / indigo / rain / yellow / lightning**.

① The colour of Sam's shorts is _____.

② A rainbow comes when the weather is _____ and _____.

③ The colour of the sun is _____.

④ In stormy weather you see _____, _____ and hear _____.

⑤ The colour of Bill the Bat is _____.

1. indigo / 2. rainy / sunny / 3. yellow / 4. rain / lightning / thunder / 5. purple.

89

Complete the address book with the 10 clues.

Clue number one
Clue number two
Clue number three
Clue number four
Clue number five
Clue number six
Clue number seven
Clue number eight
Clue number nine
Clue number ten

The address book

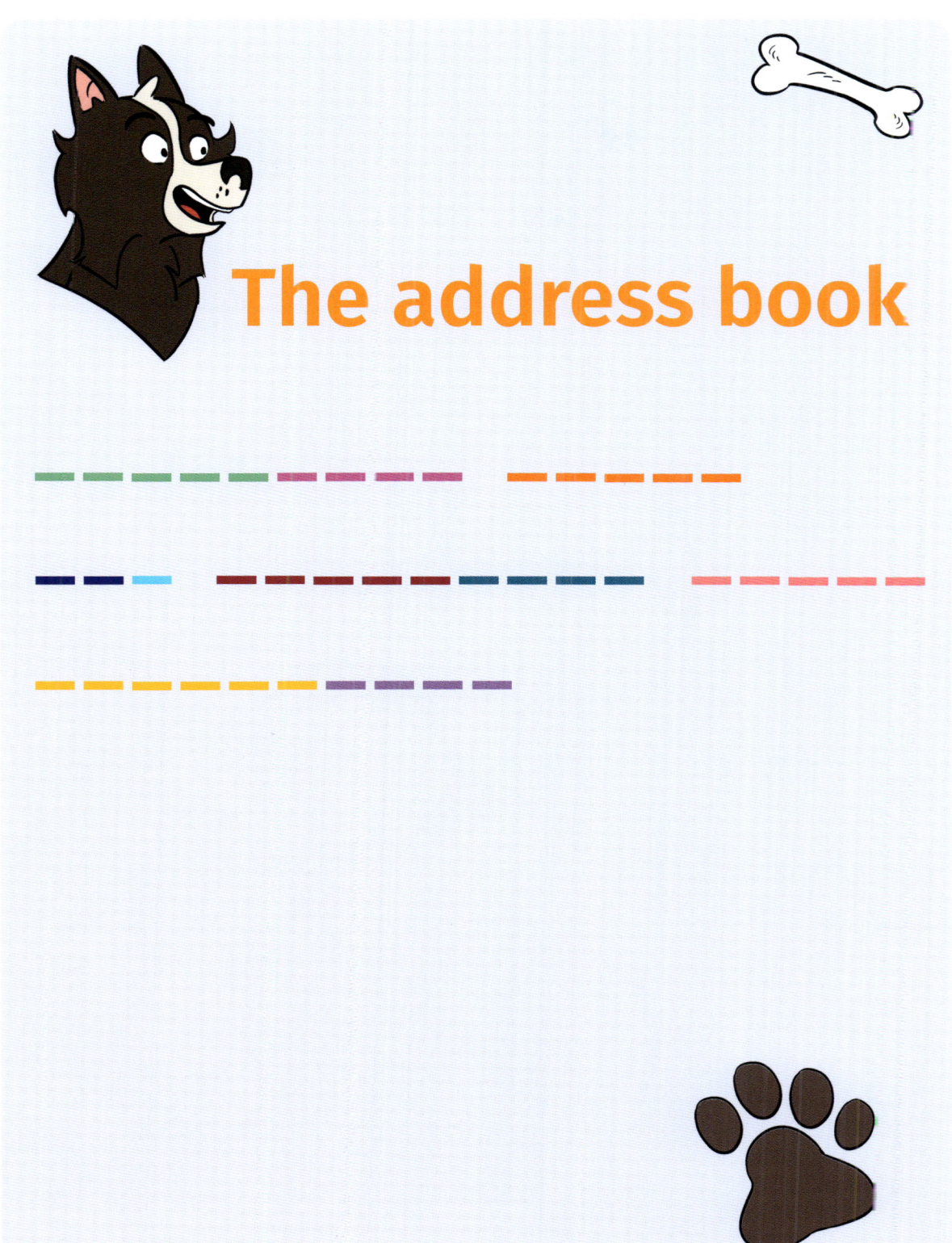

Great!

Yippee!

© 2023 Assimil
Conception et réalisation : Okidokid - www.okidokid.fr
Mise en pages : Charlotte Morin
ISBN 978-2-7005-0939-7
Achevé d'imprimer en Pologne par Drukarnia Dimograf en août 2023
Numéro d'édition : 4285
Dépôt légal : septembre 2023